CATS
IN MAY

DOREEN TOVEY

summersdale

CATS IN MAY

Elek Books edition published 1959
Bantam Books edition published 1993

This edition published in 2006 by Summersdale Publishers Ltd.

Reprinted 2007

Summersdale Publishers Ltd
46 West Street
Chichester
West Sussex
PO19 1RP
UK

www.summersdale.com

Printed and bound in Great Britain.

ISBN 10: 1-84024-497-6
ISBN 13: 978-1-84024-497-7

Also by Doreen Tovey:

Contents

ONE

Seen Him on Television?

It was stupid to write about those cats, of course. All it did – like getting their names in the Sunday papers – was make them worse than ever.

In the old days when people stopped to talk to us over the cottage gate the cats usually disappeared immediately. Particularly if they thought anybody wanted to talk about *them*.

Got a mouse to catch, Sheba would say, marching determinedly up the garden when people pleaded for a closer view of the dear little Blue Siamese. Going for a Walk, roared Solomon, beating it rapidly into the woods when somebody remarked what a big man he was and did he bite? Wasn't coming back Ever, he would add when people committed the unforgivable insult and asked – as they often did, because he was so big and dark and Sheba so small and silvery – whether he was her mother. Often after the visitors had gone I would go after him into the woods and there he'd be, sitting forlornly under a pine tree as only a Siamese can – wondering, he said sadly as I heaved him over my shoulder and carried him back to the cottage, whether to go and live with the foxes or join the Foreign Legion.

Fame changed all that. Any time anybody stopped to talk to us now, even if it was only the coal man asking whether he should come through the front gate or the back, within seconds they would materialise from nowhere. Sheba streaking down the path in a cloud of dust, skidding to a breathless halt on the wall to ask coyly whether they had read about her, Solomon swaying round the corner on long, languid legs to assure anybody who was interested that he had written it all himself.

How that cat could do it I don't know. Every single sentence of that book had been written – unless I locked him out of the house, when he sat on the garden wall gazing at passers-by with sad blue eyes and telling them that he was unwanted, or shut him in the garage where he sat and screamed blue murder – to the accompaniment of Solomon leaping round the place like an overgrown grasshopper, saying the typewriter was bad for his nerves.

I felt like a criminal every time I used it. Sometimes, indeed, seeing him stretched out on the rug with the firelight playing on his sleek cream stomach and his great black head pillowed blissfully on Sheba's small blue one, I would sneak upstairs and tap out a few lines in the spare room rather than disturb him. It was no use. Solomon, deaf as a post when he was in the woods and I, trying to get him in, was rushing up and down the lane yodelling 'Tollywollywolly' like something out of *Autumn Crocus* (it was the only call he would answer and the fact that it made people look at me rather oddly and back rapidly up the lane again was no doubt his idea of a huge Siamese joke) – Solomon, when it came to typewriters, had ears like a hawk.

One of our neighbours, long used to our cats peering nosily through her windows to see what she was doing and even, on occasion, marching in procession through her cottage from front to back, had an awful shock one day when she looked up from a spot of one-finger typing on her husband's portable to see Solomon on her windowsill leaping up and down like mad. She rang me at once in a panic. He'd gone nuts at last, she said. (There was no need to ask who, of course. The whole village had been anticipating it ever since he was born.) Would I come and fetch him, or should she call the Vet?

She could hardly believe it when I told her it was just his reaction to a typewriter. In that case, she said, why didn't he go away? Why stand on *her* windowsill jumping round like a circus flea? Why indeed, except that it was typical of him. Creep silently to the spare room or the kitchen; even, as I did on occasions, slink out, typewriter in hand, to the potting shed – and after a couple of minutes Solomon would appear, gazing at me in sad reproach and, every time I touched a key, leaping several feet in the air.

Even after I'd shut down the typewriter in disgust he still went on doing it. Move a foot – up he went like a rocket. Lift the coal-tongs – somebody, he said, turning a full circle in mid-air and landing defensively on the bureau, was After

Him. One day after a typing session the Rector spoke to him unexpectedly from behind, as he was drinking from a flower vase on the hall table, and poor old Sol was so scared he nearly hit the ceiling. It cost us a new noiseless typewriter to overcome that foible, and if anybody accuses us of being silly about animals I can assure them that it wasn't bought on Solomon's account, but because by that time Charles's and my nerves were so bad we were going round like grasshoppers too.

By the time the book came out Solomon had forgotten the typewriter, but we hadn't. When we were asked to take them to a Siamese party in London we turned green and refused on the spot. Solomon's nerves were bad, we said, and so were ours. If we took him on a train we'd be lucky to get to London in one piece. Bring Sheba, they said. But we couldn't do that either. Solomon, left on his own even for half an hour – as we knew from the time Sheba's boyfriend bit her on the tail and we had to rush her to the Vet for treatment – sat in the hall window so that the whole village could see how we were neglecting him, and howled the place down.

So we went to the party on our own and that was how the trouble started, because there we met some cats who did know how to behave themselves. A dear old Siamese queen called Suki who, judging from her crumpled ear and battle scars, had been hell-on-wheels in her day but sat there looking placidly out of her frail wickerwork cage as if she were Victoria herself. Bartholomew and Margharita, two sleek young Seal Points from Chelsea who drank sherry and looked so much like Solomon that in the midst of all the gaiety my heart sank like a stone thinking of what *he* was probably doing at that very moment – either ripping up the stair carpet or broadcasting *basso profundo* to the whole village that we'd gone away and left him. And, most impressive of all, Tig, who'd come straight from being televised at Lime Grove.

Tig was very like Solomon too, except that – though his mistress looked rather harassed and had her hat over one eye in the normal way of Siamese owners – he himself was as calm as a cucumber. When she produced his earth pan saying she hoped nobody minded but he'd been too busy up till now and it wasn't good for him to go all that time with a full bladder he looked at her with disdain. Didn't *have* a bladder, he said, strolling off to greet the pressmen and photographers as to the manner born. And sure enough, though every time we saw his owner she was looking more and more worried and still trailing him anxiously with his little pan, such was his self-control that the whole evening Tig, as became a public figure, firmly declined to use it.

I was green with envy as we rolled home on the train that night. All those cats behaving like society's top ten, even down to Tig's superb refusal of the earth box... Tig himself, suave, controlled, self-assured, actually appearing on television... What, I asked Charles wistfully, did he think would happen if our two were ever asked to go on TV?

Probably be quite all right, murmured Charles, relaxing blissfully in his seat and prepared at that moment to view anything – even Siamese cats – through a champagne-coloured haze. Probably we (which meant me) made too much fuss about taking them places. Our cats, he said, patting his headrest affectionately in lieu of Sheba's small blue rump before he fell asleep, would absolutely knock 'em on TV. Which explains why the next day, when the BBC rang up to say they had heard about the party and the book and what about Solomon and Sheba going on a programme that night, we, without a second thought, said yes.

It was a mistake, of course. I realised it the moment I put down the receiver and saw Solomon watching me with dark, Oriental suspicion from the doorway. It was a habit of his when I was on the phone and though it no doubt sprang from curiosity as to what on earth I was doing talking to myself, and probably a firm conviction that I was mad and if he hung around long enough I might do something interesting, the sight of him sitting there like some character from a Limehouse thriller sent a nervous shiver up my back.

It was a well-founded shiver, too. The moment Charles brought the cat baskets in through one door ready for the journey, Solomon, hastily abandoning his role of Fu Manchu, put his ears down and marched determinedly out through the other. By the time we had cornered him – flat under the bed yelling he wasn't going any place, it was winter and we *knew* he never went anywhere in the winter – and hauled Sheba down from the top of the wardrobe where she had gone not because she was scared but because she wanted Charles to chase her too, it was obvious what our television appearance was going to be like. Complete and utter bedlam.

It was too. Mercifully by the time we arrived at the studio – what with my nerves, Solomon gnawing frantically away at his basket like an outsize termite, and Charles, the effect of the champagne having worn off, informing me dramatically as we drove through the night that if those damned cats made a fool of him in public he'd be ruined, that was all, absolutely ruined – I was practically in a coma. What I do remember of that night, however, will haunt me till I die.

It rises before me now like a horrible dream. The procession through the foyer with Charles carrying Sheba, me carrying Solomon, and – from the look on his face that was something the BBC *hadn't* thought of – an assistant producer gingerly carrying Solomon's earth box. The briefing in the studio, with the producer practisedly arranging what I should say and where I should sit while I grew hotter and hotter thinking of what might happen when the baskets were opened. The awful moment came when they *were* opened and, in a matter of seconds, that quiet, dignified studio was transformed into a merry-go-round with Charles and the producer belting in furious circles after Solomon, who was going it like a racehorse and still shouting we knew he never went anywhere in winter. The nightmare intervals when they caught him, thrust him feverishly into my arms and, in voices hoarse with anxiety, implored me for Pete's sake to *hold* him this time. And the paralysing climax when, with Solomon's claws stuck in my back like grappling hooks, Sheba smirking complacently at the camera from my lap and the producer praying aloud in the control room, we went on the air – to be greeted, of all the damfool opening remarks, by an interviewer saying he understood I had the cats in the studio with me that evening.

What happened after that, beyond Solomon leaping from my back with one deafening yell and heading for a ventilator,

I never knew. I gather I said something about him being able to open the refrigerator, because next day two old ladies turned up to watch him do it. Sheba obviously gave her usual smug account of herself because we had a letter from a woman offering to adopt her. 'Dear wee thing,' she called her, not knowing that the one and only time we'd got Solomon to settle on my lap for half a second the little perisher had nipped him surreptitiously in the rear and set him off again like a rocket.

I dimly remember, too, Charles driving us home again, pounding his forehead with his clenched fist and asking brokenly why it had to be him, *him*, that these things happened to.

I didn't really recover consciousness till the next day, however. Next day – when the Rector came to see how I was and ask after Solomon, for whom, he said, it must have been a terrible, terrible ordeal. At that moment, Solomon hove into view. Not cringing, cowed or shaking with fright as one might have expected, but lounging loftily along with what was soon to be known as his Rex Harrison walk. He greeted the Rector with a loud bass bellow as he came up. Had he, he enquired airily – pausing in the doorway so that we might get the full effect, while behind his glasses the Rector's eyes grew round as a pair of poached eggs – seen him on Television?

TWO

Up Drains and at 'em

There must, said Charles, pulling the lavatory flush and listening despondently to the hollow gargling noise that responded immediately from the washbasin, be a reason why things happened to us.

I knew exactly how he felt. The things that had happened to us that week included Solomon being bitten by a kitten, the pressure cooker blowing up and now, as a last straw, the drains going wrong.

The immediate reasons were obvious, of course. Solomon got bitten because, having cornered a stray kitten about the size of a flea and settled down for a spot of mild torture – which consisted of sitting about two feet away, where the kitten couldn't get at him and dabbing at it inquisitively with a long black paw – he'd discovered it was even more

19

exciting to put his paw in the kitten's mouth. Twice he'd done it successfully. From the rakish set of his ears as I shot up the lane to the rescue it was obvious he'd decided it had enormous possibilities and he wasn't half feeling brave. The third time, just as I got there, the kitten shut its eyes, screwed up its courage, and bit.

Solomon, after that, had gone lame for a couple of days. Not that there was anything really wrong with him. It needed a magnifying glass even to see the bite. But Solomon believed in making the most of things. If he'd been bitten, then he was wounded. And if he was wounded – boy! were people going to know about it. The result was that when he sat, he sat with the savaged paw raised ostentatiously and trembling like a leaf. When he moved, he didn't limp like any ordinary, normal cat, he went round in anguished, three-legged leaps like a frog – which was, of course, the immediate reason for the pressure cooker blowing up. I got so unnerved by his hopscotching all over the place that one morning I put the cats' rabbit in the cooker and forgot the water; the only consolation being that when, with a loud bang, the safety valve blew out, Solomon stopped being wounded for the first time in days and went up the nearest tree like a rocket.

The immediate reason for the septic tank going wrong was, according to Sidney, who did the garden for us in his spare time, equally simple. We took too many baths. It was all very well for him, of course. Not only was he unlikely ever to take too many baths, as we realised full well when he stood to windward, but in his part of the village he was connected with the main drainage. Not officially, mind you. He would have had to pay for that.

Sidney, having constructed a quite magnificent bathroom in the corner of his kitchen, had burrowed under the flagstones on a couple of dark winter evenings when his neighbours were watching TV, risen like a trout to a mayfly under the very spot where what he referred to as th'old stink pipe passed his cottage, and quietly connected himself to it without more ado. Had he felt like it he could now take ten baths a day and it wouldn't have mattered a hoot. As it was Sidney didn't believe in baths – weakening, he said they were; all he wanted was the bathroom itself, like they had down in the Council Houses. We, on the other hand, having cut our baths to a minimum which Charles said made him feel an outcast even to think of, had only to pull the flush and – to the delight of the cats, who immediately rushed into the bathroom and began bawling threats down the wastepipe – we got these horrible gurgling noises and the cover rose alarmingly on the inspection trap.

When it got to the stage where when we poured water down the kitchen sink it immediately came up again in the bath Charles said we must do something about it. Normally, of course, Charles is not nearly so precipitate as this. When he took all the door handles off for painting, for instance – even though, as the inner side of the fastenings were latches, people were continually getting locked out and having to let themselves in again with skewers – it was months before he put them back on again. Rome, he said, while people battered furiously on doors all over the cottage and swore never to come again, wasn't built in a day, and renovating it – particularly painting six ring handles with black enamel – took time.

It was different with the drains. When they went wrong a visit from Charles's Aunt Ethel was only a week away and Aunt Ethel being what she was – a ripe old tartar, as our neighbour Father Adams described her the day he heard her carrying on because Solomon had autographed her nightdress case with large muddy footprints, and he wouldn't be married to she for ten quid – something did have to be done about it.

Unfortunately when we rang up the builder he said he couldn't come for a fortnight and the outcome, which I try not to remember, particularly at night when I lie in bed thinking of Charles and the cats and trying desperately to count my blessings, was that Charles and Sidney did it themselves.

Charles has been responsible for a good many catastrophes in his time. There was the time he fixed new wall-lights in the hall, for instance, and in a series of experimental connections produced first the interesting result that when the switch was pressed, though nothing happened in the hall, all the sitting-room lights went on; secondly, after a little adjustment, the equally interesting phenomenon that when the switch was pressed every bulb in the house exploded; and lastly – if this didn't fix it, said Charles, emerging triumphantly from the cupboard with a large screwdriver in his hand, then nothing would – the grand finale where, when he pulled the main switch, with one almighty bang all the lights in the valley went out.

There was also the time when he built a dry-stone wall which looked solid as a rock while he was doing it – at least four old men, with their eyes on a pint at the Rose and Crown, said it was the best bit of walling they'd seen since they was lads and 'twas wonderful seeing the old craft revived – and the moment the last of them tottered rheumatically round the bend of the hill the wall immediately fell down and blocked the road for hours. As for Sidney – when I reveal that, some years back, the Post Office men came out and spent nearly a week putting the local telephone wires underground and no sooner had their little green van disappeared in the direction of the big city than Sidney, who was working then for a neighbouring farmer, rode happily out with the plough and cut clean through the cable, you can imagine what the pair of them did with the drains.

First, having taken the cover off the inspection trap, they dug a long, deep trench across the lawn to find the soakaway. Then, on the advice of Father Adams who happened along just then and, though he favours an earth-closet himself, knows quite a lot about such things, they dug a long deep trench in the opposite direction and found it. Next they blocked in the pipe. After that, with a lot of sweating and straining and telling me what hard work it was, they enlarged the soakaway and filled it with stones. It was a pity that by that time Father Adams had gone home to his lunch, because he might also have told them it was silly to unblock the pipe before they got out of the trench. As it was, just as I went out to call them in to feed there was a yell from Charles, who in imagination was obviously engaged in some mighty damming operation on the Frazer River, to Let Her Flow, a biff on the pipe from Sidney's pickaxe – before you could say Jack Robinson the pair of them were ankle-deep in filthy black water and all Charles could say when I asked him what on earth he was doing was that one of his gumboots leaked.

Everything went wrong after that. While we were having lunch Solomon went out, started to poke nosily under the planks they'd put over the trench for safety and immediately fell in. No sooner had we got him out than Charles, busily cleaning out the pipes with rods – not that there was any need for it, but he said he liked to see a job well done – lost the plunger. And no sooner had we fished *that* out than there was a strangled scream from Sidney who, having been skipping merrily round the open inspection trap for hours, had just measured it with a rod and found it to be seven feet deep.

He went home shortly after that. Never in his life, he said, had he come across one deeper than four foot six before. Only have to fall down there, he kept saying starkly from the other side of the lawn, and they'd never get thee out again. It was fruitless to point out that, while that was true in principle, the trap was only about two feet square and the only way he could fall down it would be stiffly at attention, with both arms at his sides. Sidney had had enough. Home he went, looking back at us fearfully as he pedalled up the lane as if we were a couple of Sweeney Todds bent on his end, and leaving us to finish the drains the best way we could.

Spurred on by the thought of what Aunt Ethel would say if the dishwater came up in the bath while she was in it, we did. There was an interesting sequel in that, while the drains worked perfectly while the trench was open, the moment it was filled in the water immediately started going up and down the wrong pipes again like mad, but it righted itself within the week. Meanwhile – just to make sure he never had any rest, said Charles savagely; just to make sure, what with the drains and Siamese cats and blockheads like Sidney, that he was hounded till he died – the night before Aunt Ethel's arrival, Sheba disappeared.

If it had been Solomon we wouldn't have been surprised. Solomon was always turning up in odd places. Staring inquisitively through people's windows, slinking sinisterly round people's chicken runs – though in point of fact if a day-old chicken had so much as looked him in the eye he would have run for miles. One day a couple of hikers, coming past the cottage and seeing Sheba sitting on the car roof smirking lovingly at Charles, asked us if we owned a black-faced one as well, and when we said we did they said if we wanted to know where *he* was, he was two miles up the valley lurking in the long grass. Frightened the life out of them, they said he had. There they were having a quiet little picnic by the stream and Lil had only turned to throw the banana skins into the hedge and there was his great black face peering at her out of the cow parsley and she was so scared she'd spilt the thermos all over her shorts.

'Oughtn't to be allowed,' said Lil's husband tenderly mopping a stray trickle of tea off Lil's tub-shaped thigh. 'Ought to be kept in a cage,' he yelled after me as I started up the lane at the double. Pretty well everybody who knew Solomon had said that at some time or other, but that wasn't why I was running. There were foxes in the valley and while I would have bet any money on Sheba being more than a match for any fox *she* met, I could equally well imagine Solomon being dragged down the nearest foxhole still asking whether they'd seen him on television. As it happened, I met him that time the moment I rounded the corner, doing his stateliest Rex Harrison down the middle of the lane and complaining loudly because the visitors hadn't waited for him. He was safe enough. It was Sheba who, only a few days later, we were to mourn as taken by a fox.

It was an evening such as we had spent hundreds of times before – pottering in the garden, with the gnats biting sultrily and occasional oaths and the sound of breaking glass coming from the corner where, instruction sheet in hand, Charles was putting up his own greenhouse. Solomon had had his bottom smacked for rolling in the paeonies; Sheba for stalking Father Adams's bantams. Solomon had stunned a wasp and been prevented from eating it in the nick of time. Sheba, always out for effect, had stretched herself in a Diana-like attitude in a seedbox on the garden wall, causing quite a sensation among passers-by and an even greater one with Charles when he discovered she was lying on his lettuce plants. An ordinary, normal evening. Until the moment when I went to call them in for supper and found, instead of the usual bedtime tableau of two little cats sitting soulfully on the wall wondering whether we wanted them any more, only Solomon. Solomon, happily boxing midges in the dusk. His only comment, when we asked him where Sheba was, was an assurance that he didn't know but if we were worried about it he could easily eat her supper as well.

We searched for her for three hours without success. Leisurely at first, expecting to see her small pale figure come tearing down the lane or out of the woods at any moment. Then more concentratedly, with torches, looking in outhouses and old barns, tracking and calling endlessly through the woods while Solomon – locked in before he could decide to do a Stanley act and vanish as well – wailed reproachfully at us from the kitchen window.

At one o'clock we went to bed. Not to sleep, but to wait for daylight so that we could go on searching. It was one of the most miserable nights I have ever spent in my life. Not only on account of Sheba, who by this time I imagined a mangled little heap in some fox's den. On account of Charles, who lay there holding forth alternately on the fox which he was going to kill with his bare hands when he caught it and a mysterious perambulator he now remembered being pushed up the hill at dusk, and the more he thought of it the more certain he was, he kept telling me, that Sheba had been in it being kidnapped. On account also of the perishing gale which blew round the bed like Cape Horn and was the result of having every door and window in the house wide open so that we could hear if she called. And not least on account of Solomon, who at two o'clock started howling his head off in the spare room.

'Poor little chap,' said Charles when, after a particularly piercing scream we decided we'd better have him in with us before he woke the entire valley. 'He's missing her too,' he said as Solomon, with a reproachful sniffle, marched in and peered suspiciously under the bed. He wasn't, of course. All Solomon was worried about was whether we'd had Sheba in with us and not him. When he discovered she was nowhere to be seen he snuggled happily down with his head on my shoulder and within a few minutes was snoring like a pig. A little later the snores gave way to the steady grinding of teeth. Dreaming happily of being able to eat all Sheba's suppers in future as well as his own – and drowning, incidentally, any chance we had of hearing her footsteps if she did come back – Solomon slept.

The cause of the trouble returned at nine o'clock next morning. We had been out since daybreak, combing the woods again, calling her till we were hoarse, looking apprehensively in streams and cattle troughs in case, like a small blue Ophelia, she floated there among the duckweed. Father Adams had arrived, spade in hand, with the intention of digging out the fox's earth in the wood so we might know if that had been her end. Charles, flatly refusing to believe we had lost her for ever and enlarging on his theory that – presumably bound and gagged, since we'd heard no sound – she'd been carried off in the perambulator, was on the point of ringing Scotland Yard. Solomon, with his smuggest I'm-here-aren't-I-not-silly-like-Sheba expression, was sitting conspicuously on the cooker determined not to miss anything. I, gazing dumbly at the kitchen table, was trying to realise that never again would I see her sitting there explaining earnestly just *why* she wanted more fish – usually because Solomon had pinched hers while she wasn't looking. When there was a cracked soprano wail and in she stalked.

We never discovered where she'd been. From the mud on her paws and her worn-down claws I personally believed she must have been accidentally locked in somebody's outhouse and spent the night trying to dig her way out. Sheba herself supported Charles. Kidnapped, she assured us, crossing her eyes and beaming enigmatically every time we looked at her. Locked in a cellar with iron bars and a great big man on guard. Got through a window and walked ten miles home with the kidnappers hunting her every inch of the way. Make a good story for Television, wouldn't it? she demanded, sauntering airily over to her plate to see what was for breakfast. Whereupon Solomon did what I felt very much like doing myself. Knocked her down and bit her on the bottom.

THREE

The Reason Why

The immediate reasons for the things that happened to us were indeed obvious. You didn't need to look far for the reason why people thought we were nuts, for instance, when practically every day saw us marching through the village at least once carrying those wretched cats in public procession – Charles pink with embarrassment because the only way Sheba would be carried was flat on her back in his arms, gazing adoringly up into his face; I with Solomon dangling goofily down my back like a sack of coals while I held on to him by his back legs. Unless of course it was the fly season, when, though I still held him by his back legs, with his front ones he would be flailing the air behind me like a demented windmill.

Even people who knew us – who knew that we were only fetching them back from the Rector's or the Williamses or whoever it was that had rung up to complain about them this time – looked at us a bit oddly on such occasions. People who didn't know us usually thought we ought to be locked up.

Father Adams, who owned a Siamese himself and knew what it was like – though his, he said, was pretty good these days except when our two devils led her into mischief – was quite indignant one night when somebody said as much in the Rose and Crown. 'Said he seen thee sliding out of the woods on thee backside with a dappy gert cat round thee neck,' he informed me over the gate, his voice – as was usual when he was conducting a conversation at a distance of more than three feet – a full-blooded bellow that could be heard all over the village. Probably he had at that. The wood was on a steep slope and, once having caught Solomon, the only way to get out of it without letting go of him *was* to sling him over my shoulder and slide down on my seat, with the result that, in a community where practically every female under forty wore jeans, I could be identified a mile away by a large black mudpatch on mine.

What had annoyed Father Adams, however, was the stranger's inference that I was odd, coupled with the observation that he supposed most country people were a bit touched anyway. 'I told he!' he roared, tipping the brim of his hat belligerently over his eyes like the characters he had seen on Telly when they, too, had put somebody properly in their place. 'I told he, not half I didn't!' What, I enquired wearily, for I knew Father Adams's home truths of old, exactly had he told him?

It was as I feared. Father Adams had first informed him that I weren't as daft as I looked, followed by the announcement that if he thought I were he ought to have been here a few years back. When, he had advised the startled stranger triumphantly, he'd have seen I going round with a squirrel on my head.

I am digressing here, however. What I was really coming to was that Charles was right. There was a reason – a deep-seated, fundamental reason way back behind all those immediate reasons – why things happened to us. And I knew what it was.

Sometimes, being only human, I was inclined to blame it solely on to Charles. The time the brakes froze on the car one bitter night miles from anywhere, for instance, and, having left the tools at home for safety as usual, the only thing he could think to do was light a candle we happened to have in the car and lie hopefully underneath trying to thaw them out. That was bad enough. The wind kept blowing the candle out and by about the twentieth time Stirling Moss had held it silently out from under the car for me to re-light I was so mad I could have jumped on it. What was really so dispiriting, however, was that when eventually a man did come along with a spanner and manage to free the brakes, no sooner had we coasted a few yards down the road to prove they were free than Charles said we really must go back and thank him. Before I could stop him he had put the brakes on again – and there we were, frozen rigid as before.

At that stage I leaned my head on the roof of the car and wept. If I'd listened to my grandmother, I howled, while the snow melted forlornly in my snowboots and Charles, looking nervously over his shoulder, said Sshhhh, not here, the man was *listening* – if I'd listened to my grandmother I'd never have married him.

It was quite untrue, of course. My grandmother thought Charles was wonderful. If she'd been there at that moment she'd probably have been under the car herself, button boots and all, holding the candle with him.

I remember the time, before we were married, when he called for me one night in the pouring rain with a hole in the roof of his sports car right over the passenger seat, and the hole itself stuffed with a *Financial Times*.

There he was, dressed to kill in plus fours, diamond-checked golf stockings and a white racing helmet. There he was, tightening the string that held the exhaust pipe on and adjusting the windscreen wiper. Only for effect, of course. It hadn't actually worked since Charles bought the car. The real operative system consisted of another piece of string tied to the wiper with an end dangling in through each window, and as we went along we pulled it alternately in a sort of rhythmic rowing motion.

There he was. Dangerous Living – plus fours and all – personified. If my father could have seen either the car or Charles in that helmet he would have had a fit. But Father was engineering far away. Grandma was my legal guardian. And all Grandma did was gaze nostalgically at the golf stockings and say she wished she were forty years younger.

Halfway up the street, with the pair of us pulling away at the wiper strings like a couple of Cambridge strokes, the car back-fired and the *Financial Times* descended on to my lap, followed by a gallon or so of water which had collected on the sagging roof. Even then Grandma was undismayed.

As we backed spasmodically to the front door she came running out with an umbrella. That I didn't grab it and hit Charles on the helmet there and then; that I meekly put it up inside the car, stuck the top through the hole in the roof and, with the umbrella itself tilted smartly out of the port window – otherwise, said Grandma, the rain would run down it *inside* the car and Charles would get wet – zoomed off up the road again as if I always went about in cars with my umbrella up; that I said nothing at all about the fact that I was now soaked to the stomach because, as Charles kept reminding me, he'd promised to meet old Ian at seven-thirty and we were already late... these things are of no importance at all except as evidence that even in my salad days I should have had my head read.

What is important is that there, in a nutshell, is the basic reason why things happened to us. On my left Grandma, with whom I had lived in a state of impending calamity since the day I was born. On my right Charles, with whom I was to continue in that state from the day we were married.

They had much in common, Grandma and Charles, including a passion for gadgets that were either impractical or – when handled by them – impossible. Gadgets that were impossible for them, of course, were not necessarily impossible for other people. Take Charles's electric drill, for instance. So simple that, to quote the advertisement, a child could use it. The first day he brought that home he used the sanding attachment to polish an old copper kettle I had just bought in a junk shop. Wild with enthusiasm he not only sanded a hole clean through the kettle bottom, he also – as a result of doing the job in the bathroom because he said that was the most convenient power point – turned the bath and lavatory seat emerald green in a shower of copper dust. Which, I regret to say, became embedded, and we have an emerald spotted lavatory seat to this day.

When he used the paint mixing attachment he not only mixed the paint, he went on so long that eventually the whole lot shot out in a sort of circular tidal wave and Solomon, hanging hopefully around in case we were getting something to eat, became temporarily the only Seal-Point Siamese in existence with bright blue ears. When he used the drill itself with no attachment whatever, to drill a couple of holes to fix the switch for the hall lights, he managed that all right. The trouble was he then went on to fix a switch that was – according to Father Adams – big enough for Battersea power station, with two little inch-long screws. The result was that within two days the switch came off in somebody's hand and for the next six months – until Charles, who flatly refused to have a smaller switch, remembered to buy some longer screws – the switch, with a couple of whacking great cable wires attached, lay tastefully on the hall table and anybody who wanted to go upstairs operated it from there.

Aunt Ethel, grovelling one day for the switch which had fallen down behind the table and coming up instead with a dead mouse which had been filed there by Sheba, said she didn't know how I stood it. The answer was simple, of course. This was exactly how I had lived with Grandma. Down to the gadgets which invariably went wrong. Down to the paint – Grandma had once painted some chairs, putting the second coat on before the first was dry, and for weeks when unwary visitors sat on them there had been a gentle rending sound every time they got up. Even down to the mice.

Grandma once had a cat called Macdonald who was *bitten* by a mouse. Believe it or not, she used to say, she had seen that cat one day with a mouse which had its teeth firmly fixed in his chin while Macdonald himself – one paw on the mouse's tail, his head strained upwards like a giraffe and the poor old mouse stretched like elastic in between – tried desperately to lever it off. As a result of that experience Macdonald had developed a complex about mice. When he caught them he no longer ate them, but laid them out in rows in conspicuous places and gloated over them. Visitors needed jolly strong stomachs to take tea in our house in those days, when more often than not there were half a dozen mice laid out on the rug before their very eyes and a big black cat sitting proudly by the side of them like a pavement artist, but Grandma would never allow them to be taken away from him. It would hurt his subconscious, she said. It was his way of retrieving his pride after the mouse had bitten him. If people didn't like it, she said, when any of us remonstrated with her, they could do the other thing.

We would soon have been left without any friends at all if it hadn't so happened that Grandma also had three parrots and that one day Piquita, the Senegal parrot, bit Macdonald on the paw when he was seeing how far he could reach into her cage. Piquita was always biting people. She was the most fiendish bird I have ever come across – and that, considering the number of parrots Grandma kept in her time, all of which bit at the slightest instigation, was saying something. She was small, with a green back, orange stomach, yellow legs and a grey, snake-like head. She had pebble-grey eyes which were also cold and snake-like, except when she got annoyed, when they turned bright yellow and went on and off like a Belisha beacon.

You could always tell when Piquita was going to attack by the flashing of her eyes. The trouble was, by that time it was generally too late. Her usual time for attacking was when she was being fed and, with Grandma's usual inconsistency, while her other parrots all had cages with seed tins that fitted from the outside, Piquita alone had a cage where they hooked on to the inside.

She also, lucky little bird that she was, had a door which instead of opening outwards slid vertically up and down in grooves like a portcullis. Every member of the family, with the exception of Grandma, was trapped at some time or other by that blasted door coming down on their wrist while they were putting in the seed tin, whereupon Piquita, her eyes flashing on and off like neon signs, dived down and bit them solidly in the thumb.

Grandma was as deaf to our complaints about Piquita as she was about Macdonald's mice. If she bit us, she said, we must have offended her and it served us right. Piquita, she would observe with the air of finality which she always adopted to complaints about her pets, never bit *her*. The astonishing thing was that she was right. Grandma could do anything with birds, just as she could with animals. Immediately one of us was bitten, even while we were still hopping round doubled up and sucking our thumbs in anguish, off she would sweep in great concern to comfort Piquita – and there, a couple of seconds later, you would see that horrible bird lying on her back in the bottom of the cage, wings widespread, eyes closed in ecstasy, while

Grandma tickled her on her stubbly little stomach and said what a wicked lot we were to torment her.

What with Macdonald's mice and Piquita biting life was pretty arduous for us just about then, and it seemed – to everybody except Grandma, anyway – poetic justice when in the end our two crosses cancelled themselves out.

Piquita, as I have said, bit Macdonald one happy afternoon when he put his paw in her cage, and Macdonald, no doubt remembering what Grandma was always saying about his subconscious and the need for him to retrieve his pride, subtly plotted his revenge. The rest of the day he sat licking his paw and glowering darkly at her from under a chair. That night, while we were all in bed, he marched purposefully into the sitting room, knocked her cage off its table, the sliding door which had been our own downfall so often in the past slid smoothly up in its grooves for the last time – and that was the end of Piquita. When we came down next morning we found the cage upset, birdseed all over the floor and Piquita herself laid out regimentally on her back alongside the night's catch of mice.

Grandma was inconsolable at her death. Right up to the loss of the next of her parrots, which happened a long time afterwards and was another story altogether, she never stopped mourning Piquita and saying how she was the best, most faithful, most loving parrot she had ever had. As for Macdonald, sitting up there so proudly and waiting for her to congratulate him on his night's haul – he, bewilderment in every line of his fat black face at her sudden change of attitude, got the tanning of his life and never caught a mouse again. Any time after that if he even thought of chasing a fly he would hesitate, look at Grandma, lower his ears and slink under the nearest chair. Humans, he said, gazing stonily at us out of his big yellow eyes while we stroked his ears and promised him a consolatory saucer of milk when she wasn't looking, were Horrid.

FOUR

Blondin

My grandmother was awfully pleased when Charles and I acquired a squirrel. It just showed how we liked animals, she said. I took after her, as she'd always said I would. Charles... she'd always liked Charles, and to think of his taking this dear little orphan of the woods, comforting it and bringing it up... it just *showed* how right she'd always been.

Actually Grandma, as usual, was as far from right as she possibly could be. We hadn't adopted Blondin willingly. We liked animals, yes. But squirrels – as, in those carefree, far-off days, Siamese cats – were hardly our cup of tea. All we had aspired to until then had been three Blue Rex rabbits with which Charles, fired by a book entitled *How To Make Money In Your Spare Time*, had once dreamed of founding a flourishing rabbit business. The idea was that he would sell the carcasses at tremendous profit to a shop and I – as Charles was continually pointing out, they had magnificent pelts – could have a fur coat. What actually did happen was that six months later, by which time we had a grand total of twenty-seven rabbits and they were costing us a fortune in bran and potatoes, Charles announced that he couldn't kill them. They were his friends, he said. Particularly the little one with the white foot. Had I noticed, he asked, how that one could actually climb the wire of the hutch door like a monkey when it was opened, and the knowing way it would sit up on the top tier and wait to have its ears scratched?

As a matter of fact I hadn't. I was too busy cooking buckets of bran mash and scouring the hedgerows for dandelions. One thing I did jolly well know, however, was that I wasn't going to be the one to kill them; neither could we afford to go on keeping them in rapidly expanding multiples forever. The outcome of that affair was that Charles's friends eventually departed *en masse* one Saturday afternoon on a handbarrow, hutches and all. We had sold them alive to another breeder – a small boy who informed us firmly that the bottom had fallen out of Rex rabbits, and that while six months earlier we had paid seven pounds ten for three of them the best he could do for us now for our total of twenty-seven was thirty bob, including hutches. If, he said, with a meaning glance at Charles, we wanted to sell them *alive*.

Well, there we were. We didn't adopt Blondin willingly. Neither was he the dear little orphan Grandma so imaginatively described. He was a silly clot who had fallen out of a thirty-foot high drey one cold March afternoon, no doubt as a result of his own nosiness, and when we found him he was lying at the foot of a towering pine tree. Shivering, hungry – so young that his tail hadn't even feathered out yet but was thin and stringy like a rat's; so tiny that he couldn't even crawl.

Charles having firmly refused to climb thirty feet to put him back in the drey – though many a time later he was to wish fervently that he had – the only thing we could do was to take him home with us and look after him until he could fend for himself. Contrary to my grandmother's picture of Charles comforting and nourishing him, I, incidentally, was the one who gave him a good going-over with flea powder when we got there, and I was the one who kept getting up at hourly intervals throughout the night to feed him warm milk from an Apostle spoon.

I was also the one who, when we woke next morning to the realisation that somebody was going to have to give him hourly feeds through the day as well if he was to survive, was detailed to take him to the office with me. When I pointed out that Charles's office was more private than mine, and he could much more easily feed Blondin without attracting attention, he looked at me incredulously. Who, he demanded with horror, had ever heard of a man feeding a squirrel in an office? I could have asked who had ever heard of a woman feeding one there either, but it wouldn't have got me anywhere. When I trudged tiredly into my office at nine that morning Blondin was with me, wrapped in a blanket in a shopping basket.

Actually the first day people hardly knew he was there. The milk had unfortunately been too strong for his small stomach and the whole day he lay there like a dead thing with me forcing a mixture of brandy, warm water and sugar down his throat at regular intervals and waiting for the end. The next day, however, Blondin felt much better. Halfway through the morning there was a screech like a train whistle from under my feet and when I touched ground again and looked under the desk, there was a small brown head regarding me indignantly from the folds of the blanket. Where, he demanded menacingly, rattling his teeth at me in a way I was to come to know very well indeed in the weeks that followed, was his Brandy?

There was no trouble in feeding him after that. Diluted brandy, cracker biscuits mashed to a gruel with sugar and water, Blondin took the lot, sitting up to suck at it with both paws clasped tightly round the teaspoon and refusing point-blank – all our animals showed their independence at a dishearteningly early age – to feed from the fountain-pen filler we bought for him on the second day.

His fame spread quickly once he was up and about. People came from all over the building to see him and hold his teaspoon. Others brought him pounds of nuts and were most disappointed when he didn't sit up and start eating them right away. Even the scream which meant he was hungry, and which could be clearly heard halfway down the corridor, rapidly became part of the office routine. So much so that when the clarion call sounded one morning while my boss, myself and a rather important visitor were discussing early Virginian history the only one who jumped was the visitor – and he nearly went through the ceiling. I merely streaked automatically for the door while my boss startled the poor man still further by telling him I'd gone to feed a squirrel.

It couldn't last, of course. It ended, in fact, the moment Blondin began to feel really good and realised what he was. Nobody, said one of my colleagues towards the end of the second week while he frantically tried to extricate Blondin from half-way up his coat sleeve, where he had crawled by way of experiment and was now firmly wedged and screaming his head off, could like animals better than he did – but an office was not the place for squirrels. They ruined the filing, complained the filing clerk – and indeed quite a bit of our current correspondence had an odd octagonal look where Blondin had tried his teeth out on the corners. They upset the ink, said the junior – and indeed there was a large black splodge on the carpet where Blondin, looking hopefully for something to drink, had indelibly proved it. They were bad for his heart, said the boss, leaping madly for the door one afternoon as Blondin, who had been idly chewing a pencil on my desk, loped light-heartedly across the floor and sat up right in front of it just as somebody prepared to come in. Would I please, he said, leaning against the door-jamb and mopping his neck with a trembling hand while Blondin clambered happily up his leg to thank him, take my blasted squirrel HOME?

Grandma was awfully annoyed when she heard about that. She wanted to go down and speak to my colleagues, and I had an awful time dissuading her. They'd never get on, she said wrathfully, if they weren't kind to little animals. (From what I could see my immediate prospects didn't look too good if I *was*.) Heaven would pay them out for it, she said, wagging her teaspoon vigorously in the air. Heaven would... At that moment the small tawny figure which had been busily teething on the picture rail till it spotted the teaspoon sailed gracefully through the air and landed on her head and Grandma, who wasn't expecting him, nearly swallowed her pastry fork. She changed her mind after that. What that little devil wanted, she said, wiping the remains of her cream puff from her chin and glaring grimly at him as if he were suddenly a sprig of Old Nick himself – was a cage.

For a short while, for his own good, he got one. He had by this time progressed to being able to feed himself. Not so politely as we might have wished, perhaps. At first we gave him his mash in a saucer into which, the moment he saw it, he immediately jumped and got his stomach wet. We got so tired of continually drying his stomach out on a hot-water bottle that eventually we gave him a cup turned on its side. He threw himself just as lustily into that, rolling and sucking noisily as he ate and getting himself plastered with mash, but at least he kept his stomach dry, and at least he could feed himself. So we left him at home with his basket and his cup of mash and his drinking water – and the very first day he was left alone, growing more squirrel-like with every hour that passed, he climbed on to a shelf, chewed the paint off a tin, and poisoned himself.

We cured him that time with copious doses of magnesia. We were, said Charles, hammering fiercely away that night at a large packing case which he was converting into a cage to prevent Blondin from attempting suicide the next day as well, getting to know quite a lot about squirrels. Not as much as Charles thought we did, I'm afraid, because he said a rhinoceros couldn't get out of that cage once he had reinforced it, whereas with Blondin it lasted just until the end of the week, when we went home one night to find that he had chewed a hole in a corner just large enough to squeeze his small, fat body through and was regarding us complacently from the top of a cupboard.

After that he was never put in a cage again. Fortunately he had learned his lesson about chewing tins, but he achieved other catastrophes with clockwork regularity. He went through a period of imagining that his tail worked like wings, so that he was continually launching himself into mid-air from the backs of chairs and falling flat on his face. Then, apparently having decided that altitude might help, he tried it from the top of a six-foot cupboard and nearly killed himself. Fortunately we were on hand to pick him up. His small button nose was streaming with blood and he had sprained his hind paw so that he limped for days, but after screaming hard for several minutes he calmed down, drank a teaspoon of brandy and water with the air of one who hated the stuff but knew it would do him good, and decided to live.

His next escapade was really spectacular. Through his habit of sprawling in his mash at mealtimes the fur on top of his head had become completely glued down with sugar mixture which had hardened into a glossy cap and made him look like an advertisement for brilliantine. We made several attempts at washing it off, but the gloss was immovable. Blondin himself spent hours vainly trying to comb it out with his claws, sitting up and twiddling away at his top-knot till Charles said he found he was doing it himself when he wasn't thinking. Finally, however, Blondin's patience gave out. One day while we were away he sat down and pulled the patch out by the roots. When we got home he emerged from his basket to greet us, inordinately pleased with himself and as bald as a coot.

This was before the days of Yul Brynner, and we were terribly ashamed of him. People were continually asking how he was and it seemed such an anti-climax to keep producing a squirrel who looked as if the moths had been at him. It was weeks, too, before his fur grew again – until the wrinkled pink tonsure which disconcerted everybody except Blondin himself disappeared, and he looked like a normal squirrel once more. Meanwhile he had progressed beyond the soft food stage and was at last able to eat nuts. At first they had to be cracked for him, and he had no idea of storing them, but from the very beginning there was an instinctive ritual about his nut-eating. Always, however hungry he might be, he would carefully peel three-quarters of the nut before he began to eat, spinning it round in his paws as he worked. He always held it by the unpeeled portion – and never by any chance would he eat the part he had been holding. When he progressed to cracking nuts for himself he never discarded the entire shell, but used part of it as a holder for the kernel so that there was no need to touch it at all. He ate slices of bread and apple in the same manner, always discarding the part he had held. Tomatoes were his favourite fruit – probably because the first one he ever tasted was one which he stole himself from a bowl on the kitchen dresser – and these, too, he carefully peeled before eating. But far and away above anything else Blondin loved tea. He decided that he liked it quite suddenly one morning at breakfast, while he was sitting on Charles's shoulder. Without more ado he catapulted himself down

Charles's arm and dived headfirst into the teacup which he was just raising to his lips.

The tea – fortunately only lukewarm – went everywhere. Over Charles, over the tablecloth, and over Blondin, who emerged looking as if he had had a bath, wiped his chin on Charles's dressing gown, and retired blissfully to the back of a chair to lick himself dry. After that he would leave whatever he was doing at the first glimpse of the teapot, and the only way to ensure peace at mealtimes was to give him a saucerful before pouring out our own. Only once I forgot – and when I came in from the kitchen our dear little orphan of the woods, as Grandma still persisted in calling him, was on the table, standing on his hind legs and hopefully pushing his tongue down the spout.

By this time Blondin was quite a sizeable squirrel, and perfectly able to look after himself. The only drawback to his prospects of survival when we set him free was the fact that he was, unfortunately, not the rare Red Squirrel which his sandy baby fur had led us to believe, but had developed into a perfect specimen of the American Grey – and as such he was liable to be shot at sight by anybody who saw him.

It was difficult to know what to do. He was so tame that we hated the idea of parting with him – and the fact that he was liable to be shot if he were at large surely gave us every excuse for keeping him with us. On the other hand it seemed wrong to deprive him of his birthright. If he were to be shot, at least he wouldn't know anything about it until it happened. Meantime he would have led a full life, climbing to his heart's content in the windswept trees, perhaps even finding a mate and building a drey of his own...

Finally we decided to compromise – to set him free not in his native woods but in the vicinity of the farm where we were living at the time, in the hope that we should still see him sometimes and that, as everyone in the district knew him by sight, he might escape the gun at least for a while.

So, one fine warm morning in July, we carried him to the far end of the garden and put him gently on a tree trunk. He sniffed about him curiously for a moment, his whiskers bristling with interest, his tail bushed out and fluttering with excitement. Then like lightning, he sped to the topmost branches, chasing himself giddily round and up and down, until at last he had to stop and lie out along a branch to get his breath back.

Sadly we stood and watched him, waiting until he should take it into his head to make for the taller trees on the other side of the wall and pass out of our keeping forever. But Blondin didn't go. He romped and played in the branches until he was startled by a crow flapping its way briskly over his head – then he was out of the tree, streaking across the lawn and hiding fearfully behind the kitchen door almost before we knew what had happened. He didn't like the idea of being a wild squirrel, he informed us with chattering teeth as we carried him back indoors and put the kettle on. He liked us… and tea… and sitting in Charles's pocket and sleeping in the wardrobe… He was, he announced, regarding us happily over the top of the biggest walnut we could find for him, going to stay with us for Ever.

FIVE

The Story of a Squirrel

Blondin – sometimes we wondered if it was the result of the brandy – was not an ideal squirrel. He threw nutshells and tomato skins on the carpets. He was obstinate and self-willed. When a situation arose such as his deciding to spend the evening in Charles's pocket and Charles not wanting him to, it invariably ended in Blondin getting tough and threatening to bite. Squealing with rage, battling tempestuously with his claws, peace would descend only when he was curled cosily in Charles's pocket, with – presumably it acted as some sort of radar device – his tail hanging down outside.

With me he preferred to be the other way up. He particularly liked me to wear a sweater, when he would sit inside it on my shoulder with his head sticking out of the

50

top. I cooked, I did housework, I answered the door – all with Blondin gawking happily out of my collar so that I looked like a two-headed hydra. Not, as Grandma claimed, that he did it from affection. Just so that he didn't miss what was going on.

Blondin never missed anything if he could help it. As soon as he could climb he had taken to sleeping in our wardrobe, in a pile of Charles's socks in one of the pigeonholes. There he slept the night through; snug, warm, safe from his enemies – so secure that if we woke up during the night and listened, invariably from the direction of the wardrobe we could hear small but distinct snores. As soon as dawn broke, however, Blondin was up and keeping an eye on things. Hopping up and down the bed, peering into drawers, looking out of the window at the birds and finally, with his tail curled jauntily over his head, settling down to wait on top of the wardrobe, where he could spot us the moment we got up.

Many a piece of mischief was planned from that little lookout. He was there the morning Charles looked at his watch to see the time and, instead of getting up straight away and putting it on, stuffed it under his pillow and went to sleep again. We overslept that morning, and when we did get up we had to move so fast that in the rush Charles completely forgot his watch. Not until halfway through a hurried breakfast, when we realised that Blondin was missing from his usual vigil by the teapot, did he remember it – and by that time it was too late. When we rushed upstairs Blondin had it under the bed. Cracking it to get at the tick.

He was there, too, the day Charles brought home his new suit from the tailor's. From his eyrie Blondin watched with interest, his head on one side, his tail curled into a question mark, while Charles tried it on. He also watched with interest while Charles put it on a hanger and hung it inside. We did notice that that night he went to bed earlier than usual, but nobody thought anything of that. He often popped off up to the wardrobe by himself when he felt tired, and indeed by the time we went to bed ourselves he was already fast asleep, snoring away inside his pile of socks like a small buzz-fly.

It wasn't until next morning, when Charles said it was a fine day and he might as well wear the suit, that we discovered what had made our little orphan of the woods so tired. Not only had he taken every button off the new suit, as Charles discovered when he went to put the trousers on. Overcome with achievement, he'd chewed the buttons off all his other suits as well.

There was no need to enquire which of us Blondin belonged to at that moment. He was all mine. He was always mine when he did anything wrong. The time he upset a bottle of ink, for instance, paddled in it and then left a Chaplinesque little trail over a shirt that had just been ironed – he was mine then all right. It was a wonder he and I weren't sent to the Zoo together.

He was mine, too, the day Charles locked the wardrobe to keep him off his suits and Blondin, equally determined to get back in again, chewed a large chunk out of the door. I was out at the time but it was my squirrel who greeted me on my return, chattering indignantly away on the top. My squirrel, Charles informed me, trying fruitlessly to fit the bits back in again – who, if he couldn't behave in a civilised manner, would have to Go.

Normally, of course, he was Charles's squirrel, and if he'd gone anywhere it would have been over Charles's dead body. Circumstances altered cases, too. When it was not Charles's watch but my handbag that he chewed through – a neat, semicircular hole in the flap to get at my fountain pen – there was nothing mischievous about that. It was just, according to Charles, an example of his intelligence that he should have noticed where I kept the pen and – being naturally curious about it – used his brains to get it out.

He was certainly intelligent. Young as he was when we found him – far too young to have learned anything from other squirrels – he still knew instinctively when the summer began to wane and it was time to start storing nuts. He kept his in the hearthrug and nearly drove us mad by the way he had no sooner buried them and carefully patted over the top by way of camouflage, than he got all worried because he couldn't see them and immediately dug them up again, turning them suspiciously over in his paws to make sure they were still intact.

Actually the last bit was due to Charles rather than instinct. Charles liked nuts too, and one day Blondin caught him helping himself to a particularly fine walnut he had found under a cushion. Incredulously he watched while Charles cracked and ate it – his very own nut – and never offered him a piece. Incredulously, afterwards, he examined the nutshell before he could believe that Charles, his friend, had done this thing to him. After which it was entirely Charles's own fault that whenever he entered a room he was tailed by a squirrel who leapt on guard as soon as he approached a cushion and who, the moment he went near the hearthrug, patrolled furiously up and down it threatening to bite if he so much as moved a foot.

He knew, too, all about building dreys. We had at that time a bed-settee which we sometimes used for guests and Blondin, when he felt like a nap without the bother of going upstairs, often disappeared inside it for an hour or so, going in by a private entrance of his own through the back. One day, seeing him dragging a traycloth across the floor and finally, after considerable effort, getting that through the back as well, we opened up the settee to find a sock, a small screwdriver, a dozen or so paper handkerchiefs which he had stolen from a packet in a drawer, and a good half-pound of nuts. The socks, the handkerchiefs and the traycloth had been fashioned into a snug little nest in which, when we opened the settee, he was rather sheepishly sitting. The nuts were obviously siege stores. The screwdriver – we had been searching for that for days and Charles said he couldn't think why Blondin wanted that. I could. To defend himself when Charles went after his nuts.

It was just about then that we bought the cottage. Not because of Blondin. We had been looking for one before he was even thought of – though as Charles said, it did seem opportune that we found it the week he ate the farmer's housekeeper's begonias. It consoled her a little, anyway.

It was a relief to us, too. Blondin by this time had the energy of a horse and teeth like a pair of pneumatic drills; we'd been praying for weeks that he wouldn't start in on the farm.

Now, we said as we drove down the hill to our new home with Blondin in a birdcage on the back seat, for the life we had planned. Digging the garden; entertaining our friends; quietly, selectively, getting to know our neighbours...

Not so quietly or selectively as we imagined, I'm afraid. On our first night there we gave them the shock of their lives. It began by my having a bath and turning on both taps at once. A thing, as Charles said afterwards, that anybody might do, except that in our case it caused the ballcock to stick in the tank and the tank to overflow into the yard.

It continued with Charles, already perturbed by the rate at which the water was gushing into the yard, worrying about the boiler. A strange house, he said, a system we didn't understand... heaven only knew how the pipes went in this old place. He thought we'd better take out the fire.

We did, which was why that first night our quiet country retreat strongly resembled a scene from Faust. Water pouring like Niagara into the yard. Charles and I appearing alternately at the back door in our dressing gowns carrying buckets of coals which, as soon as the wind touched them, burst spectacularly into flame. Dramatic moments when – for, so far as the onlookers could see, no particular reason at all – we pushed the buckets under the overflow with a shovel and doused them in clouds of steam...

Nobody interfered, of course. One or two cars going down the lane slowed abruptly for a moment and then, in the manner of well-bred Englishmen, drove on. Only from the gate – from a little knot of awed spectators on their way home from the Rose and Crown whose attention was divided equally between our activities and those of a large buck squirrel who was intently watching the proceedings from the kitchen window – came any comment. Just one solitary, awestruck voice. Later we learned it was Father

Adams, but we didn't know him then. 'God Almighty!' it said.

We stopped the overflow eventually by climbing into the roof and lifting the ballcock. What we couldn't stop, of course, was the talk that went on. At the farm at least people had known us before we had Blondin – and, in the manner of village life, when we did have him everybody knew why. All they knew here was that we'd arrived with a squirrel in a birdcage, that there'd been some odd goings-on in our backyard the night we came, and that we were quite obviously mad. It took us a long, long time to live that verdict down – if we ever did.

Part of the trouble was Blondin himself, of course. We were so used to him by now that except for running when we heard him chewing the furniture we took him quite for granted. Other people – even if they'd heard of him – didn't.

Sidney, nervous as a hare when he came to work for us and obviously expecting us to start doing war dances round a fire bucket at any moment, nearly fainted in his gumboots when Blondin ambled over his feet carrying a screwdriver in his mouth. The woman who called for a charity subscription – telling us over a friendly cup of tea that she had a little squirrel in *her* garden too, who ate all the wallflowers – wilted nonetheless when she reached down for her handbag and encountered the tail of *our* little squirrel, who was busily investigating its contents.

Even the bravest of them – who, when he came to supper, allowed Blondin to sit on his stomach saying this was nothing to what he'd experienced in the Colonial Service – looked a bit shaken when he got a nut stuffed down his trousers waistband and a firm refusal to let him take it out. Safe from Charles in there, said Blondin, peering down the top and patting it affectionately in place. We retrieved it in the end by persuading our visitor to stand up and shake himself, while Blondin clung chattering protestingly to his stomach, but it put rather a damper on the evening. He never came again.

When, after a succession of incidents like that, we went home from the office one night to find that Blondin had vanished, nobody was particularly perturbed. 'Gone back to the woods,' they said when we explained how he had chewed a hole under the kitchen door and squeezed his way out. 'Never see he again,' was the gamekeeper's verdict when we asked him, if he did come across a squirrel on his rounds, not to shoot it but to see first if it was tame.

We thought that he was right. Blondin was a different animal now from the little squirrel kitten who'd been frightened by a crow. Tough, powerful, well able to defend himself – what was more natural than that he should go back to the woods. Nor, in our heart of hearts, could we have wished to stop him. All we could do was to put away his nuts, move a pathetic, half-eaten apple from the mantelpiece, and wish him well.

Odd, wasn't it, how a little shrimp like that had got us? said Charles, as we peered out into the rain that night wondering if he was safe. What was odder still was that *we* seemed to have got Blondin. Two days later, when we went home from the office he was back. Huddled in an armchair looking sheepishly at us from under his tail. A self-willed, sandy little scrap who, though he'd left us at a time when the woods were ripe with nuts and for miles around there stretched more trees than the most ambitious squirrel could ever hope to climb, had of his own free will come back to us...

Maybe it was affection. Maybe it was just that two nights in the woods, surrounded by strange noises without his hot-water bottle and – worst of all – without his tea, were more than our adventurer could stand. Whatever the reason, he never left us again. For two years after that wherever we turned – unless he was asleep – there he was, swinging on the curtains, chewing at the furniture, peering hopefully down the spout of the teapot.

He died eventually, one cold, wet autumn morning of a chill. For weeks we mourned him, forgetting the mischief he had done and remembering only the fun we had had together. We tried to get another squirrel, but we never could. There were none to be had in the local pet-shops – and the Zoo, when we asked, said they had a waiting list for squirrels.

Which was why, missing the crash of crockery, overrun by mice who were looking for his nuts – and, as Charles said, definitely not in our right minds – we went in for Siamese cats.

SIX

Sidney Has Problems

Four years now we'd had Solomon and Sheba and, as Sidney put it, we hadn't half had some times with them.

We'd had a few with Sidney, too. Life sometimes seemed as full of his little problems as it was with Siamese cats and, right from the time he came to work for us, we were always getting involved.

Take, for instance, the time he was caught riding a motorbike without a licence. There was nothing we could do about the offence itself. Even Sidney admitted it was a fair cop. His friend Ron had offered him a run on his new model; Sidney, with a quick look round for P.C. McNab, had jumped on and tried it up the hill; McNab, to quote Sidney's own description, had immediately leapt from behind the phone box like a blooming leprechaun – and there he was. Two pounds fine and no licence for a year.

What worried Sidney, and was where we came into the story, was that he'd just started courting a girl who lived ten miles away. Bit of all right she was, he advised us after his initial date, and the prospects were looking so favourable that he had in fact decided to go in for a motorbike himself, which was why he had been trying out Ron's. And now, he demanded the day after his appearance in court, where was he? Leaning on our lawnmower as a matter of fact, where he'd been moored for the last half-hour, informing us soulfully that he didn't suppose we'd feel much like courting either if we had to do ten miles on a push-bike first.

We saw him through that little crisis, as he no doubt hoped we would, by running him over to Baxton ourselves on courting nights. There being a limit to what we'd do for Sidney, he had to make his own way back. There was one night, alas, when he didn't even get there. A dear old lady who'd known him since childhood said she was going to Baxton – she for once, would take Sidney to his tryst – and when the silly old fool turned up, said Sidney next morning, she had a blooming great dog sitting in the passenger seat, he couldn't get the rear door open, and to his astonishment, while he was still wrestling with it, she had suddenly said 'Quite comfy, dear?' and driven off.

She was deaf, so the fact that Sidney hadn't answered didn't register. She also drove with her nose glued to the windscreen – like ruddy Lot, said Sidney, getting quite incoherent when he thought about it – and it wasn't until she rattled into the square at Baxton that she realised he was missing. Given her a terrible fright, she said it had, imagining poor Sidney having fallen out en route, which was nothing to what it gave Sidney when he imagined Mag waiting by the Baxton turnpike, him not turning up, and – at this point in his ruminations the mower went straight into the paeonies – her perhaps going off with some other chap.

As a matter of fact she didn't. Sidney had far more fatal charm than anybody realised. Eventually he married her, honeymooned triumphantly – the penal year being up – on a brand new motorbike, and became the father of twins.

Even that failed to cheer him up, however. He still worried about things. When the Rector caught him sawing logs for us one Sunday morning, for instance – Sidney hid in the woodshed when he saw him coming, and when in spite of this precaution the Rector looked round the door and asked him how the twins were he was terribly worried about that. Bet th'old sky pilot had him down in his little black book now, he said, wrestling gloomily with his conscience after the event. It was no good our trying to comfort him, either, with an assurance that the Rector was broadminded – that he judged people by their principles and wouldn't really mind. Sidney knew a parson's duties, and he worried even more. Then he ought to mind, he said.

He worried when the twins kept him awake at night. How long, he enquired – and some mornings, indeed his eyes looked exactly like a panda's – could a bloke *go* without sleep? He worried when he thought he was losing his hair. Actually Sidney's straw-like thatch never had been very thick, but once he persuaded himself it was going there was no end to the worrying he did about that. The day he arrived having flattened it down with water that morning, to see, he said, how he'd look when *'twas* gone – we had to give him a glass of sherry to pull his nerves together

What raised this particular incident to epic proportions was that unfortunately everybody, when they heard about Sidney's hair, started giving him remedies. 'Bay rum,' said one – whereupon Sidney arrived smelling more pungently than the Rose and Crown. 'Paraffin,' said somebody who knew a travelling hardware man who always rubbed his head with his hands after serving oil and *he* had hair like a child – after which we had to be jolly careful not to strike matches when Sidney was around. 'Goosegrease,' advised somebody else – at which stage Sheba announced that she didn't love Sidney any more and Solomon, going round the kitchen like a mine detector, said he reckoned we had dead mice in here.

It passed eventually, like all Sidney's worries, but it was pretty trying while it lasted. His next one took a different turn altogether. Mag, he said, wanted a fur coat. Seen one in some magazine, she had – picture of some girl wearing one when she went shopping and she thought 'twould be nice when she went to town. Sidney, sweating at the thought, had already tried diplomatic tactics. Told her she'd look daft in one of they in the sidecar, for instance, which didn't impress her a bit. Left his newspaper with us on the days it carried those spectacular full-page fur advertisements – whereupon she went next door and borrowed the neighbour's. What, he asked – absentmindedly eyeing the cats, whereupon Sheba took *her* fur coat up the garden in a hurry while it was still safe – did we think he ought to do now?

He found the answer himself that time. We could hardly believe it when he zipped down the hill on his push-bike on the following Monday – whistling, his cap perched jauntily on the back of his head and his feet on the handlebars for good measure.

'Got Mag her fur coat on Saturday,' he announced, rubbing his hands triumphantly as he stamped into the kitchen for his cocoa. 'Where?' we asked in chorus, scarcely daring to think what the answer might be. 'Jumble sale,' he said, with a last man-of-the-world drag on his Woodbine before he flicked it through the kitchen door. 'Got her a smasher for ten bob.'

Sidney wasn't the only one who had problems. Father Adams, for instance, was in trouble with his wife over a faux pas about our cats. Very proper was Mrs Adams. Always out to do things right by village standards. Doileys under the cakes, doileys under the flower vases, smart chromium fruit spoons – to the annoyance of Father Adams who was apt to ask what the hell was this for and what was wrong with his teaspoon – when visitors came to tea. Always out to improve Father Adams, too, which was why she was so pleased when the hunting gentleman came by.

We were leaning on the gate at the time, lazily discussing with the Adamses the prospects for the harvest supper, and when the vision in hunting pink and fine white breeches came clopping down the lane and not only stopped but raised his top hat to us she was nearly beside herself with pride. He enquired after Solomon and Sheba. He had read about them, he said. He had seen them on television… There was no need for further conversation. At the mention of their names Solomon and Sheba appeared as if by magic.

Not obtrusively, seeing that we were all so busy talking. Just side by side across the lane and – so that nobody could possibly think they were showing off – with their backs to us, their tails raised in concentration, intently studying something in the hedge.

'Solomon and Sheba,' indicated Charles, thinking the visitor might like to see them – as indeed he did. 'Well, well, *well*,' he said, gazing at their rear views in admiration. 'Solomon and Sheba! The dear little chaps themselves!'

It was calling them little chaps that did it. Father Adams, seventy years a countryman, was astounded that a hunting man could show such ignorance. 'Cassn't thee tell even from this end?' he said.

How, asked Father Adams miserably after the horseman had gone and Mrs Adams had stalked in prim dudgeon up the lane, were he going to put *that* right? I didn't know. I had troubles of my own at the time. Charles was being a handyman again.

Inspired by an article in a do-it-yourself magazine he had started redecorating the kitchen. And half-way through redecorating the kitchen – leaving me with three pink walls, one dirty cream one and five cupboard doors which he'd taken off for painting and left propped against the wall for the cats to play tunnels through – he'd got inspired by another article and started paving the yard.

Even that wouldn't have been so bad – it certainly needed doing, Sidney said he'd help him, and between them they might, with luck, have finished it in a month. But unfortunately Charles decided that while he was at it he would do the thing properly, with drainage. A simple, Y-shaped system, he said, with rainwater pipes running underground from either corner of the cottage and ending in a soakaway inside the back gate. And that was where Sidney resigned from the scheme. Yards was all right, he said firmly, but he was hoping one day to get his pension, and he had the twins to think of. He weren't digging no more soakaways for *us*.

So Charles, undaunted, set out to do the job himself. Very well he did it, too, as far as it went. Two professional-looking trenches converging towards the centre, filled in as he went along and with the paving, flat and smooth as a spirit level could make it, growing before our very eyes. He was just past the water-butt when the thought struck him that pretty soon it would be tree-planting time, and that the site for the fruit trees he'd ordered back in the gay, carefree days of summer wasn't ready yet.

'Another hour at this and I'd better start digging the holes,' he announced one morning, swinging his pickaxe practisedly through the air. He was as good as his word. An hour later, with four more feet of trench opened, drainpiped – but not, seeing that the allotted time was up, filled in again – Charles departed to dig holes up on the hillside. Unfortunately it is rather stony ground up there. Very difficult indeed to find a depth of soil sufficient to take fruit trees. A week later, when a card arrived to say the trees were now ready and when would we like them delivered, Charles was still delving feverishly away on the skyline.

The kitchen remained unfinished. One night, when we had some special visitors coming, he did get around to putting the doors back on the cupboards. Unfortunately he didn't put the screws back in the hinges – what was the point, he said, when he'd only have to take them off again as soon as he started painting? He had, in fact, merely tucked them in for show. A fact which, full of bonhomie, I forgot when the visitors were actually there, and when I opened one to get out the coffee cups the damned thing fell down and nearly brained me.

Despite my apprehension the trench, too, remained unfilled. Charles said the main thing was to get the trees in, and the yard was a job he could do in the winter. Only an idiot could fall down that little hole, he said, when I suggested perhaps we should put a plank over it in case of accidents.

He fell down it himself the next night, coming through the gate in a hurry. The neighbours were always having narrow escapes, particularly as the weeks went by and the nasturtiums spread across the gap. And Solomon went down it practically every day, chasing Sheba round the garden for exercise.

That, of course, was funny. It was obviously deliberate, too, from the way his big black head peered through the nasturtiums a second later, waiting for the laughs.

It wasn't funny, though, the night we heard a crash and a howl and rushed out to find the baker in the trench. Not our regular baker, who knew the route through the nasturtiums and was a nice little man with corns and three children, but a rather unfriendly substitute who had, he informed us as we helped him out, already done a full day's round and was doing our end of the village because his mate was sick. What did we think we were up to, he demanded as we dusted him down and handed him back his basket. Catching ruddy elephants or trying to break his neck?

Charles filled in the trench before breakfast next morning without a mention of the fruit trees. He did say now he'd have to leave the soakaway till Spring – to which Father Adams, leaning reflectively on the gate to watch him, said 'twas just as well. Somebody might fall down there afore then, he said.

SEVEN

And So to Spain

Something, said Charles, would have to be done about those cats. He said that quite regularly. It came in jolly handy for changing the subject at times, particularly when there was a slight suggestion in the air that something ought also to be done about Charles.

Like that very morning, for instance, when, moving a large bottle of pickling vinegar out of the way with his foot so that he could get on with sandpapering the kitchen wall, Charles had knocked it over and smashed it. With speed born of experience – Charles had knocked quite a lot of things over in his time – he had immediately locked the kitchen door. With speed also born of experience I nipped quietly round the front, in through the back door which he hadn't thought of locking – and there, sure enough, was

Charles gingerly pushing a cloth round in a sea of vinegar with his toe.

Not that he was at all perturbed when he was caught out. All he said, lifting the sopping cloth expertly towards me on the end of his shoe, was that this one was wet now and could he have another. Even when, breathing fire and slaughter, I wrung it out and got down to the job myself he was quite undaunted. Wonderful how vinegar brought the tiles up, wasn't it? he said admiringly as I mopped away. If I asked him we'd made a discovery there.

We'd just made one about Solomon, too, which was the cause of his latest remark about the cats. At that moment there was a car parked outside our garden wall with its occupants gazing absolutely entranced at Solomon, who was apparently giving a solo ballet performance on the lawn. He leapt, he pranced, he postured – every now and then adding a variation where, for no apparent reason, he lay on the ground and stuck his paw down the clock-golf hole.

'Dancing nicely, isn't he Mummy?' asked a small treble voice through the car window after one particularly effective pas de seul. To which Mummy replied – sadly, for obviously she liked cats – that she was afraid the poor little chap wasn't feeling well.

Solomon was all right. He was just showing off with a mouse. The reason his audience couldn't see it was because it was about the size of a mothball and the reason for that was that he had caught it himself. It was one of the few he had ever caught – the only size, alas, he was ever likely to catch. Even that had taken him a whole morning of sitting on a mole-hill in an adjoining field gazing hypnotically at a clump of grass – at the end of which, if we knew anything about it, the poor little mouse had had to come out or die of starvation and Svengali had probably fallen on it and squashed it flat.

Not that that worried Solomon. Even if it was only a moth he captured he went round like Trader Horn. Even when he couldn't catch anything he still showed off.

Lately he'd taken to hunting under the blackberry hedge in the lane. Being Solomon it was naturally the most inaccessible hole he wanted to look down – and being a mug where he was concerned, I naturally helped him. Time and again I was caught by passers-by holding up the brambles for him while he explored underneath, either poking down the hole with his paw or else, which looked even more impressive, sitting intently by it waiting for his quarry to come out. Time and again people stopped to watch, obviously expecting – what with him and me and the raised brambles – that something big was about to be caught at any moment. And time and again after collecting his audience and keeping them on tenterhooks for ages, Solomon got up, stretched, and strolled nonchalantly away.

Who was it who looked sheepish then – who dropped the brambles as if they were red-hot, muttered something about it being a nice day and slunk embarrassedly through the gate? Certainly not Solomon. Nothing large enough today, he assured them airily from the garden wall. Not even a snake bigger than three feet long. Come again tomorrow, and see what we caught *then*.

Sheba's attitude was just as bad. She had perfected a method of putting us in our place which was effective in the extreme. Any time we refused to let her out, or her supper wasn't ready, or she was just plain fed up, she sat in front of us, eyed us witheringly, and sighed. It was the sort of sigh my maths mistress used to give when she saw my geometry homework, and I knew quite well what it meant. It was even more demoralising coming from a Siamese cat.

Added to that Sheba, when she was out these days, didn't come home when she was called. One word from me, or even from Charles whom she normally obeyed as promptly as if she was his Eastern slave, and she was off up the lane like a shot.

Her goal was a neighbour's strawberry bed up on the hillside. He was – as she was doubtless aware, seeing that she passed several other equally good strawberry beds to get there – the one man in the village who objected to my trespassing on his land to fetch the cats; everybody else's attitude was that I could get the so-and-so's any way I liked, so long as I removed them fast.

So there, if she made it first, she sat in her sanctuary of strawberries while we yelled threats at her from the lane and she bawled companionably back. Sooner or later somebody would come by and ask why didn't we go in and *fetch* the little dear, not shout at her like that. And the moment we tried to, as sure as eggs were eggs, out would pop the old man shouting one foot in his strawberries and he'd sue us while Sheba, having achieved her object of reducing the neighbourhood to bedlam, melted quietly from the scene and went home.

Something certainly would have to be done about those cats. The question was… what?

Somebody suggested we got another kitten. That, they said, would take them down a peg or two and keep them in their place. Our answer to that – little knowing what fate had in store for us in that connection – was that we weren't quite as crazy as that yet. Not only were the trials of bringing up our own two still shatteringly fresh in our minds, but we had examples enough of what happened to people who had kittens.

There were the friends who owned Chuki, for instance. We'd warned them ourselves what to expect if they bought a Siamese. So, to be quite fair, had the owner of Chuki's mother. When they went to see her she said sometimes the only way she kept from going mad was to go for a long, long walk and, when she came back, give that cat a darned good hiding. It made no difference. They still bought one. All it needed, they insisted, was patience and a firm hand, and with an intelligent little thing like that there'd be no trouble at all.

The last we'd heard of them they were thinking of moving. Three months they'd had him. In that time he'd wrecked the furniture, eaten a hole in an eiderdown, nearly been built into a compost heap and got himself locked up at the police station for vagrancy. Not in an ordinary cat-cage, either. Got hisself out of *that* like Houdini, in an hour, said the sergeant. When they went to fetch him home – his report sheet said he'd been found wandering in the street at 1 a.m. and picked up by a patrol car – he was sitting triumphantly in a cell.

Added to that their left-hand neighbours weren't speaking to them because he kept going in and frightening the baby and their right-hand neighbours were complaining about the state of their garden. They were looking, they informed us in their last sad phone call, for a place in the middle of Exmoor or the Sahara, where he could operate without landing them in jail as well.

If, as somebody else suggested, we'd thought of adopting an ordinary kitten – just to take the edge off them, they said, and so much more *manageable* than a Siamese – we had the example of the Rector to put us against that. Recently – inspired, according to him, by the devotion of our own two cats – he had acquired a couple himself. Not Siamese. Solomon had once fallen out of a tree on to his head and nearly frightened him out of his rectorial collar, and the inspiration didn't go as far as that. His kittens were Hardy, a sleek black tom, and Willis, his charming black and white sister. Most appropriate they looked too, sitting in clerical dignity on top of the Rector's wall – until one day he noticed they were developing rather big ears.

He couldn't have been more alarmed if they'd started sprouting horns – and with equally good cause. Since Ajax, the doctor's Seal Point tom, had been brought over to mate with Father Adams's Mimi he had developed rather a penchant for our valley. Nowadays we quite often met him sauntering hopefully down the lane – and if, following her operation, Mimi herself was no longer interested when he called, there were other cats who were.

His progress through the valley was like Alexander's march through India – in Ajax's case littered not with fair hair and Grecian noses but with kittens with big ears. They also inherited a marked propensity for trouble. Three of them were already locally notorious. One who was privately owned had eaten six fish out of a fishpond; one at the Post Office had torn up some postal orders and eaten the stamp account; and one at the garage was refusing to let dogs get out of cars. *His* place it was, he said belligerently; all his including the petrol pumps, and he'd do them if they did.

It was to guard against such a contingency happening to him that the Rector got his kittens from a farm three miles up the valley – but it was no use. Ajax, he said, gazing at Hardy and Willis despairingly while their ears practically grew before our eyes, had progressed further than he thought. He had indeed. Faithful to their ancestors, developing their heritage in a style suitable to their surroundings – Hardy had so far been sick on a canon and marooned on the church roof and Willis had bitten the curate's hat.

By the time we went on holiday we still didn't know what to do about our pair. We'd had one idea that had helped a little. We'd bought them a tortoise called Tarzan, and for a while that really seemed to work.

It was wonderful to look out of the window, see them slow-marching with Tarzan across the lawn, and realise there was no need to shadow them – that ten minutes later, even if we wanted to go to town, they wouldn't be on the other side of the village or chasing somebody's chickens round a field. Just a few inches further on, peering intently under his shell.

It was marvellous to find that bringing him indoors at night obviated the yelling and wrestling that usually went on. That instead of pushing one another off the bureau or Solomon howling because Sheba was looking at him they were peacefully side by side under the table, united as a team of research scientists and still looking under his shell.

It was cute, too, to see them when it rained. Sitting in the porch watching with interest while he pottered across the grass and taking it in turns, when he stopped, to rush out into the downpour, make sure his engine was still under his bonnet and, with a few encouraging prods to his rear, start him moving again.

So cute, in fact, we failed to realise he wasn't half getting some exercise for a tortoise, and when one day, taking advantage of the cats being in for lunch, he nipped athletically up the path and disappeared we were taken by surprise. We couldn't find him anywhere – not even helped by Solomon. Neither could we replace him. By that time, according to the pet shop, the tortoise season was over.

So, promising ourselves that next year we'd get another and keep him on a leash or something, we gave up the search and went to Spain on holiday. Parking Solomon and Sheba once more at the cattery and determined to enjoy ourselves.

We did too, except for one or two little mishaps. Like my ordering iced beer en route at Biarritz, for instance, and getting – even the waiter looked surprised when he brought it – beer and ice cream. Like Charles losing his shirt at San Sebastian, which is typical of the way things happen to us. One minute we were sunbathing on the beach saying how peaceful it was and why couldn't life always be like this, and the next the tide had swept in, whipped it off his chair and carried it out to sea. And there was everybody getting excited and shouting, the beach policeman looking fixedly at Charles and twirling his walking stick – because there is a rule in Spain about men going round without shirts on – Charles marching back to lunch trying to look nonchalant in a towel and everybody laughing... All it needed to be just like home was the cats bringing up the rear. There was, too, the affair of the Prado. We'd already had one or two little difficulties with the language. Like Charles going into the shower at our first hotel, for instance, pulling the chain marked *Calido* – thinking, he said, as any sane and normal person would that it meant Cold – and nearly going through the roof when it turned out to mean Hot. Like our deciding to see a *pelota* match and running like mad up and down the front at Santander – to discover, far too late to see the encounter, that the *frontone* mentioned on the placards didn't mean the front at all, but was the place – like golf course in English – where they actually played the game.

By the time we got to Madrid we'd given up going by guesswork or trying – Charles's favourite occupation – to work it back to the Latin. We'd got ourselves a phrase book and a map. Which was how, not being at our best at reading town-maps, either, we came to make the mistake about the Prado.

Emerging from the Metro into the Plaza de la Cibeles, struck by the majesty of his surroundings – the magnificent statue of the lady with the lions, the imposing splendour of the Alcala Gate and the notice which said Paseo del Prado – Charles, who is himself something of an artist, grew suddenly solemn. Impressively he marched me into the tremendous building on the corner. Rose-coloured, Gothic – housing, he informed me as we respectfully mounted the steps, the finest art collection in Europe. He'd have known it anywhere.

The trouble with me is I always believe him. Walking on tiptoe, scared almost to breathe in this hallowed Mecca, I was just about to ask the way to the Goyas when I noticed that the people leaning confidently over the polished counters were not, in fact, getting information about pictures. We were in the Madrid General Post Office. They were buying stamps.

EIGHT

Fire Down Below

No sooner had we returned from Spain than Charles caught the chimney on fire – which was one way, at any rate, of letting people know we were back. The Rector said as soon as he heard the fire engine he guessed we were home again.

It was a pity really, because it was the result of the first spring clean the bureau had had for years. Sorting through the post that had accumulated while we were away Charles had stuffed most of it in a pigeonhole, hammered the top down to show it who was master, and was just turning away when the hinges broke and the cover fell off.

Something, he announced, surveying the avalanche of papers, catalogues and home-handymen magazines that poured like a mountain torrent on to the floor, would have to be done about this. Whereupon – refreshed by his holiday, filled with a determination that from now on things were going to be more orderly around here – he did it. Threw one or two catalogues on the fire, mended the hinges with a couple of paperclips, shovelled the rest of the papers back in through the top, went to bed – and next morning we had a phenomenon. No fire in the grate, but from the garden the cottage appeared to be steaming up the valley like the *Queen Mary*.

We caused some excitement in the village that day. First on the scene was the postman, who said some people did have 'em didn't they and advised us to call the brigade. Next came the milkman, who said if he was us he wouldn't. His cousin was in that lot, he said, and he knew what they'd be like if they got going. Hoses down the chimney. Fireplace wall knocked out before we could look round in case it was a beam. Ladders straight through the roof of the conservatory we'd just put up at the side of the cottage – damfool place to build he too when you come to think of it, he commented amiably, swivelling his head back towards Charles. If he were us, he said, he'd get somebody local to sweep the chimney first in case 'twas only burning soot – and *then* if it didn't stop fetch out the brigade.

Close on his heels we got a small boy in a cowboy hat, standing on our gate with his trousers nearly falling off with excitement. And finally, thanks to the milkman who'd obligingly made him his next port of call, we got Father Adams. Carrying a set of brushes and determined to do it himself.

I tried to dissuade him, but it was no use. He had a tale about the fire brigade too. Didn't want what happened to his sister Minnie up in Essex did I? he demanded sternly. Called 'em because her oil stove caught on fire, rushed out to meet 'em when they came, door slammed behind her – and before she had a chance to tell 'em the back door was still open, he said, dropping his brushes dramatically in the fireplace, they had their hatchets out and was going at it like kangaroos!

I didn't. Neither, on the other hand, did I want Charles and Father Adams sweeping the chimney. But that was what I got.

Tempers became a little frayed during that operation. Father Adams got a bit touchy when, having sent Charles out to see if the brush was through the pot – because, he said, he'd now screwed on fifteen rods and if our chimney was that high he was a Dutchman – Charles came back to report that it was not only out, it was drooping over the roof like a dying sunflower, with a whole crowd of people watching it from the lane. Silly lot of bs, said Father Adams, hauling it in again as fast as he could. Serve 'em right if it fell on their silly great heads and knocked their silly great brains out.

I didn't exactly howl with laughter when he and Charles went up on the roof and poured a couple of buckets of water down the chimney for safety's sake – carefully stuffing a couple of sacks in the grate before they started so the water wouldn't run out into the room, then marching triumphantly back removing the sacks, and letting it.

And Charles was quite stricken when I complained. For heaven's sake what was a drop of water compared to having hearth and home on fire? he demanded striding manfully through it in his gumboots to peer up the chimney and see if it was all right now.

Nothing at all. Except that two hours later just when I'd got it all cleaned up and was wondering if I had the strength for lunch, hearth and home caught on fire again.

We got the brigade that time. All it was was soot – caught by burning paper – smouldering on a ledge halfway up the chimney, and all they did, after checking it with a mirror, was brush it off with special brushes and hose it down. After a cup of tea, and comforting us with the information that in about five years the ledge would build up and probably catch on fire again but not to worry, just ring the old Brigade, they went. Leaving us, if you counted ten and took a broad, calm, practical view of things with hardly any more mess than when Charles and Father Adams did it the first time. As Charles said, at least we knew it was well swept.

It was wonderful, after all that, to be driving down to the cattery next day to collect the cats. Good old English air, said Charles, taking deep breaths of it as we went along. Good old Sol and Sheba. Didn't it seem marvellous to be fetching them home again?

It certainly did. Always, when we were going on holiday, we spent the last few days beforehand saying if we had to put up with them a moment longer we'd go clean round the bend. Always, when we drove down to Halstock with Solomon howling sorrowfully in his basket and Sheba apparently reciting poetry in hers, we said if we had to listen to them for another mile we'd go mad. And always, the moment we got back to the empty cottage and saw the poignant little reminders of their life with us, we felt unaccountably sad.

There were so many little reminders. The marks on the sitting-room wall, for instance – juicy and slightly spattered – where Solomon caught gnats on summer evenings. Similar marks in the spare room where Sheba, not to be outdone, sat on top of the door and slapped her lot to death on the ceiling. The staircarpet – new last year, but you'd never have thought it; not after four happy little pairs of feet had given it an all-over mohair effect and in one spot, on the top tread, two happy little pairs of feet (Solomon's) had ripped a hole clean through to the underfelt. The bath, which if it were cleaned ten times a day (and sometimes it very nearly was) could still be depended on to have a trail of footprints wandering nonchalantly round the edge and, at the bottom resemble nothing so much as an elephants' waterhole...

By the time I'd done a tour of remembrance, emptied their deserted earth boxes and put away their feeding bowls I was practically in tears. By the time we were actually *on* holiday, with distance lending enchantment as, oddly enough, it always does with Siamese cats, we saw them as perfect little angels. We could hardly wait to get news of them – to make sure they hadn't pined or caught chills or died of sorrow. Which, since we never booked our hotels in advance and the people who kept the cattery had to write to us Poste Restante, added a few more complications to life.

Whatever else we miss when we go abroad we certainly know the Post Offices. There is one in Florence, under an old grey arcade, which we haunted so persistently I swear they took Charles for Dante's ghost. There is one in Heidelberg where, when the polite young man said '*Nein*', we went down to the river – Solomon and Sheba were five months

old then and we were sure they'd died of broken hearts
– and mentally threw ourselves in. There is one in Paris
which smells – or it did when we were there last – distinctly
of over-ripe cheese. Where, holding handkerchiefs to our
noses, we argued for days that there must be a letter for us,
and when it did arrive the clerk was so relieved he shook
hands with us under the grille...

The message, of course, when it did find its way to us,
was always the same. 'S. and S. well, eating like horses and
not missing you a bit.' After which, feeling as if Mafeking
had been relieved, we went and had a drink.

It *was* nice coming back to the cats. Even when we turned
in at the gate of the cattery and heard two familiar voices
busily bellowing the place down we didn't flinch. Even
when we saw they weren't the homesick little creatures
we had envisaged – when Solomon stalked the length of
their run to inform the Siamese in the next chalet that if he
said *that* again he'd dot him one, and Sheba lay happily in
Mrs Francis's arms informing us she was staying on here
because she liked the food – we were still glad to see them.

What with the fire, all the sun we'd been having and this
absence-makes-the-heart-grow-fonder business, we were
in fact in that bemused state of mind in which people *buy*
Siamese cats. If anyone doubts that there is such a state I
can only quote the case of someone I knew – in her fifties,
she was; an old maid living alone whose only interest was
taking care of herself. She went to bed every night at half-
past eight even when she had visitors (if they over-stayed
she politely sent them home). She rested for an hour after
lunch with her feet up and a bandage over her eyes to keep
out the light. And her house was so spick and span that

every ornament in the place had a little felt mat under it, cut exactly to shape, to prevent it marking the furniture.

If she wasn't bemused when she bought a Siamese I don't know who was. Something came over her, she said, when she saw his little black face mewing pathetically at her through a pet-shop window. Actually he wasn't mewing but bawling away like a town crier, as she realised when she went into the shop and got on the same side of the glass. Something had certainly come over her, though. She bought him just the same.

She doesn't go to bed at half-past eight now; she's still trying to get Lancelot in off the tiles at ten. She doesn't rest after lunch – she can't, she says, for worrying what Lancelot is up to. She doesn't have little felt mats under her ornaments any more; she hasn't got any ornaments. What she has got is Lancelot. And – though admittedly she worships the ground he strolls on – she still doesn't know how it happened.

If that could happen to her you can imagine how we were affected when, going into the Francises' kitchen for coffee that night before our journey back, we were confronted by an entire family of Siamese kittens.

Entrancing it was, to people who either didn't know Siamese or – like us – were still suffering from the Spanish sun. Kittens dangling from the door handles. Kittens diving off the stove. One sitting thinking by a saucepan and another blissfully asleep in a little doorway cut in the cupboard under the sink.

That, explained Mrs Francis, hauling him out while two more who had been queuing outside dashed precipitately in, was the way into their earth box and he wasn't asleep at all, he was doing it purposely. That, she said, as there was a resounding crash from upstairs followed by the sound of a wardrobe apparently being trundled across the room and pushed through a window, was another lot playing with a rabbit foot. Locked in her office, as they were a slightly older family, to prevent them from murdering this set.

If there was a sort of despairing note in her voice just then we never noticed it. We were too busy dreaming a happy dream of one of those dear little kittens installed in our own cottage. Not for our own sakes, of course, but for Solomon and Sheba.

Give them a kitten, we said enthusiastically as we drove home in the car that night, and it might reform them on the spot. Give them something to think about – to protect and cherish and play with – and it might be the making of them. Maybe, said Charles – choking slightly as Solomon, finding a fresh hole in the basket, thrust his paw through it, hooked Charles expertly in the hood of his duffel coat and pulled – it would even cure Solomon of *this*.

It was unfortunate that in the course of conversation the Francises had mentioned that all their kittens were booked. If they hadn't, when by the following weekend we had decided quite definitely to adopt another kitten, we should have gone to them for one. They knew a lot about Siamese psychology, and they also knew Solomon and Sheba. They could have told us it wouldn't work. That an orang-utan was about the only animal we could put with those two, for instance, and expect it to survive. Or, as Charles said on Sunday night in a mood of deep despair, suggested that we had our heads read.

As it was, hardly able to wait to have a dear little kitten around the place again, we got one from another breeder. From a very nice lady who said his name was Samson and wouldn't that be *sweet* with Solomon and Sheba, and who asked, as we packed him into Sheba's basket (which was the only intact one we had) if we would mind taking him to bed with us for the first night or two. In case, she said, blinking back a tear at the thought of parting with him, to begin with he felt lonely.

She wouldn't have worried about that if she'd seen the reception our two gave him when we took him in. Asleep they were. Curled affectionately together in a chair before the fire. With, as we entered, two heads – one big, beautiful and black, one small, intelligent and blue – coming up in a loving, cheek-to-cheek pose that a photographer would have given his pension for. She wouldn't have worried if she'd seen the way the next moment, with an incredulous sniffing of the air, they were on their stomachs, ears flat, whiskers bushed, fighting ridges raised on their backs – creeping across the carpet like a pair of special agents.

She wouldn't have worried either – not about where he slept, anyway – if she'd witnessed the spectacular scene when they reached the basket. When they crouched down one at each end like a pair of snipers and hissed long, warning hisses through the air holes – while Samson, the moment the lid was raised, gave one despairing hiss back and leapt straight into the air.

As Charles said, standing on a chair and trying desperately to unhook him from the curtain rail while our two informed him from below that if he dared set foot on *their* carpet, in *their* house – in *their* valley, roared Solomon, his tail lashing from side to side like a whip – they'd eat him. As Charles said, she'd have had a fit.

NINE

The Great Siamese Revolution

Samson at first sight reminded us very much of Solomon. He had the same big ears, the same big feet, and the same aggravating swagger when he walked. He had the same old bounce, too. Our initial glimpse of him, when the breeder opened the door to us that wet September night, had been a small white streak hurtling across the hall, passing us like a petrol advertisement a clear foot off the ground, and disappearing with a roar into the darkness.

That, said the breeder, while five other kittens peered suspiciously at us from behind her ankles, was Samson showing off. He'd be back as soon as she closed the door, she said. He didn't like the dark. And sure enough – Solomon all over, said Charles emphatically when he heard it, and we weren't having that one – as soon as the door was shut there was an ear-splitting wail from outside and Samson, screaming the place down to keep off the spooks, had to be let in again.

Samson, after that scare, had to use his box. Not with reticence, like a normal kitten, but importantly, to show what a narrow escape he'd had. Samson after that again – obviously he was already used to visitors – had to climb the ironing board. It was behind a heavy curtain in an old strange house and when he reached the top and without warning a curtain-clad object swayed out into the room – and, as he changed position, swayed silently back again – there was no need for his owner to tell *us* not to laugh. We turned quite pale on the spot.

Samson was so like Solomon that we wouldn't have had him at all except for one thing. We wanted a tom – and he was the only tom of the lot. We wanted a tom so that when he grew up he would, we hoped, be able to stand up to Solomon on an equal footing. Most important of all, we wanted a tom so that Solomon wouldn't get ideas. Adopt another she-kitten – give old Podgebelly the idea he had a harem – and, as Charles said, even if he couldn't do much about it, he'd never stop showing off. On his back with one each side washing him – that would have been Solomon. Head on one and feet on another when he slept. Knocking 'em down like ninepins when he felt like it – the way he knocked Sheba down now, only more so on account of the effect.

So we had Samson – and it was just as well we did. If a she-kitten had had to endure the treatment Samson suffered in the days that followed, I doubt if she'd have survived at all.

Sometimes I wonder how I survived myself. The first night, remembering our promise, we took Samson to bed with us, and while he spent all night on guard on the tallboy – hiccuping at intervals because they'd frightened him at suppertime into swallowing a piece of rabbit whole – the other two howled like timber wolves under the spare-room door. The second night, to even things up a bit, we shut Samson in the sitting room with a hot-water bottle and took them to bed with us – but that didn't work either.

By that time Solomon and Sheba, having failed to persuade us to put Samson in the dustbin, were ostentatiously not speaking to us. And, so that we shouldn't overlook the fact, instead of curling up at the bottom as she usually did Sheba insisted on lying and sighing heavily on my shoulder while Solomon, determined not to be done out of his usual perch, huddled morosely on top of her.

Solomon was heavy, and the upshot of that was that every time he moved or I eased my arm Sheba stopped sighing and spat. Every time that happened Solomon got down and sulked under the bed. Every time he did he jumped down with such a sad, dejected thud that he shook the floorboards and woke Samson, who immediately started to wail downstairs. What with spits, thumps, wails and every now and again Solomon's sad, self-pitying sniffles as he crept dejectedly back to bed, life certainly reached a low ebb that night. Only towards dawn, with Sheba still sighing and Solomon still sitting miserably on her head, did I doze off – and the moment I did the alarm clock went off, Sheba spat once more, and I, racked to breaking point and scattering cats in all directions, leapt clean out of bed.

It would have been bad enough if it was only at night we suffered – but by day it was even worse. The silence affected us as much as anything. For four years now we had lived to a continuous accompaniment of cat noise. Cats bawling to go out. Cats informing us that they had come in. Cats yelling because they were locked in cupboards – or, if it was Solomon's voice, anguished and coming from an unnatural level, because he'd once more attempted his ambition to go out through the transom window and, having made the jump upwards, was as usual too darned scared to jump down.

Even when we had settled down for the evening and things were normally quiet, with Charles and me reading and Solomon dreaming of blackbirds on the hearthrug, Sheba was usually nattering away. Giving us a running commentary on what she could see out of the window, sitting in the coal scuttle threatening to use it if we didn't let her out – or, when all else failed, sitting bolt upright in front of Charles, serenading him in a small, hopeful monotone, and every time he acknowledged her, giving a loud and loving squawk.

What with that, the sounds of happy conflict when they fought each other for the hot-water bottle at bedtime and the noise, common to all Siamese, of a demolition squad at work any time they were left alone upstairs, the silence after Samson came was quite uncanny. Particularly since the impression was not, oddly enough, of a house suddenly without cats, but of a house absolutely swarming with them.

I'd no sooner see Solomon sniffing sadly round the kitchen for crumbs (he'd always eaten them anyway, but it made a jolly good act to pretend he had to, now we had Samson, or Starve) than I'd pass him on the stairs. I'd no sooner leave him there, gazing wistfully after me with a look that indicated he didn't suppose he'd be with us much longer but he hoped I'd remember him when he'd gone, than I'd find him under the bed. And no sooner would I get up from there after a vain attempt to coax him out (the look that greeted me then was the one where he had reached the end of the road and was just going to sit there and Die) than he'd be back in the kitchen again, with Charles shouting up had Solomon had any breakfast because he'd just stolen all the ham.

Sheba was just the same. She went round the place so fast – scowling simultaneously at Samson from behind the clock and the top of the curtain rail, peering from behind chairs and glaring – or so it seemed – from all six shelves of the bookcase at once – that sometimes there appeared to be dozens of *her*.

As for Samson – he apparently had roller skates. One minute he was climbing the hall curtains, the next he was the bump travelling mysteriously round inside a just-made bed. One minute he was industriously eating his cereal on the kitchen rug so that he could grow up a big strong cat and hit Solomon, and the next – my heart nearly stopped beating when I discovered it – when I opened the refrigerator he was in there. For the Same Purpose, he informed me, looking happily up from a leg of chicken and adding that at this rate he'd soon be a match for old Fatty. At this rate, I corrected him, hauling him speedily out – it was obvious that another of my little tasks in future would be to search the refrigerator for Samson before closing the door – we'd soon be having him with cherries on top for dessert.

Unfortunately Samson was like this only when we were alone. In the early morning, for instance – when Solomon and Sheba – who presumably imagined we kept him in the garden overnight – rushed out through the front door the moment they were up to see if he had gone. Samson then was as we first met him. Zooming round the floor like a bumblebee (all Siamese have their peculiarities and this was one of his). Travelling up the insides of the curtains – which was obviously another, though as we didn't keep the ironing board behind them the effect was never the same. Clambering hungrily on to the breakfast table from one chair and, as soon as he was pushed down, vanishing for a few seconds and appearing undaunted on the next. When, realising that we were beaten, we covered the milk and the butter, huddled protectively over our plates and let him do his worst, Samson even talked.

This, he would say – piping away in his shrill seagull voice as he nipped under my elbow to get at the bacon or dodged expertly through Charles's guard to lick his egg – was fun. If he could only stop having those nightmares about a big cat who walked funny and a blue one with crossed eyes he'd be as happy as could be. Then he would have a thought. They *were* nightmares weren't they? he would ask, sitting suddenly down on the table to stare at us with round blue eyes. We didn't have cats like that here *really*, did we – or if we had, we'd send them away now he'd come?

There was never any need to answer. By that time Solomon and Sheba, having cased the garden like a couple of bloodhounds and found no trace of him, had had a thought themselves. By that time they were on the windowsill. Glaring in at him with narrowed eyes and fiendish expressions that practically sizzled when they saw him eating *their* liver and licking *their* plates. Samson, when he asked his question had only to follow my gaze to the window to see whether they were nightmares or not. One look at them and, with a short, sharp prayer to his guardian angel, Samson was gone.

It should have been obvious to us then that it would never work, but still we struggled on. Sometimes, for a change, the silence of the jungle war that was being carried on all round us was broken by shrill, tremolo screams which meant they'd got Samson in a corner and could we please rescue him quick, they were going to hypnotise him. Sometimes by loud, indignant wails which meant that Solomon had been so busy out-flanking Samson he'd got himself in the corner by mistake and now Samson was looking at *him*. When we heard spitting it meant Sheba was around. Not necessarily spitting at Samson. It could quite easily mean Solomon was under the table and Sheba was spitting at him.

Sheba was so mad these days she didn't care who she spat at. She spat at us, she spat at Sidney, she spat at the milkman. Most of all, however, apart from Samson, she spat at Solomon. Whether she decided that as they were so alike they must be related we never knew, but Solomon, creeping round these days like misery on wheels, left home twice and had to be fetched back from the woods.

Samson left home twice, too. The first time we found him up an apple tree with Solomon sitting a few feet below and Sheba, growling angrily at the bottom, threatening to saw it down and do the pair of them. The second time, with Samson missing and Sheba slinking back down the lane with her back up, I dashed off after him only to be informed by the small boy I met halfway up that he'd shot him. It was the one in the cowboy hat, armed this time with a catapult, who seemed these days to be in on all our misfortunes. If he had, I assured him, tearing on up the lane, I'd come right back and shoot *him*. *And* his grandfather, whoever he was, I yelled as a tearful voice called after me that if I did he'd tell his Granfer.

I didn't discover who Granfer was that day. Samson – shot, fortunately, only in Wyatt Earp's fertile imagination – was still alive. Almost out on the main road, with his fur stuck up like a crew cut to scare off wolves and his small black tail hoisted to give him courage. Determined, he said – trembling like a leaf when I picked him up, and struggling to get away – never to come back again.

But for Charles Sheba would have had a jolly good hiding when I got home. There was no doubt that she had deliberately driven Samson away. There was no doubt, either, of her rage when she saw him again. She spat so hard when we went in she nearly blew her teeth out.

Once and for all, I said, shutting Samson in the hall for safety, that cat would have to learn her place round here. It was Charles who said she didn't mean it. It was Charles who, in spite of the fact that she'd done nothing but spit at him for the past week, gathered her lovingly into his arms and said she was his little friend. It was, I am afraid, nothing but poetic justice that in the battle that took place a few seconds later, Charles was the one who came off worst.

Solomon, who all this time had been sitting in the yard eating the bacon rind I'd thrown out for the birds (he never touched it in the normal way but it came in handy now he was practically Starved, particularly when it pitched between the paving stones and he could put on a heart-rending display hooking it pathetically out with his paw) suddenly ambled in. He was an absolute genius at appearing at awkward moments – and he'd certainly chosen one this time.

Sheba – eyes crossed, hackles up, wild with fury at the reappearance of Samson – took one look at him as he came in, leapt from Charles's arms and charged. Solomon, scared nearly out of his wits, rushed for the hall door – only to find it was shut and Sheba had him cornered. In less time than it takes to say, the cat fight of the year was raging in our sitting room, with Charles and I trying desperately to part them and Samson screaming his head off in the hall.

Sheba won the first round. She bit Solomon on the paw. Sheba also won the second round. As I dived to separate them she bit me in the hand. The third and final round went unquestionably to Solomon. As Charles, grabbing the first piece of cat he could find, hauled him bodily from the fray Solomon – back to the wall and frenziedly battling everything in sight – caught him a clanger on the nose.

TEN

The Defeat of Samson

We were a sorry sight as we trudged up the hill next morning to fetch the papers. Charles with sticking plaster on his nose, I with sticking plaster on my hand, and Solomon limping three-leggedly along in the rear. Like the Retreat from Moscow said the Rector, opening his window in greeting as we passed, and which of us was meant to be Napoleon?

Alas, it was no laughing matter. Charles, from what I could gather, was expecting to die of blood poisoning at any moment. Back in the cottage Samson, quivering like an aspen, was locked in our bedroom for safety, while Sheba – vowing vengeance on everybody and, from the peculiar bumping noises we could hear when she stopped for breath, apparently busy dynamiting the airing cupboard – was imprisoned in the bathroom. We only had Solomon with us because when he saw us starting out he'd roared so hard about his foot and leaving him to be massacred we were afraid somebody might call the police. Now, as Charles said disgustedly, he was putting on such a show limping along behind us somebody'd probably call them anyway.

Charles was thoroughly annoyed with Solomon. Particularly the way he was showing off. Who hit him on the nose he'd like to know? he demanded as we passed the Post Office, and why the hell couldn't he be *carried* like a normal cat, if he was hurt? Whereupon for at least the sixth time since we started out Solomon, one paw suspended pitifully in the air, stopped to inform him reproachfully that it was an Accident, he'd meant it for Sheba, and if we were ashamed of him exercising his poor, bitten foot we'd better put him in a home.

It was at that point in our affairs that Dr Tucker came out of the Post Office and asked what was the matter. He wasn't our personal doctor, but he did happen to be the owner of Ajax. And as he said, what with the pair of us patched with plaster and Solomon howling his head off in the middle of the road he certainly knew a Siamese crisis when he saw one.

So we told him. All about the sulking and the fighting and Sheba being Guy Fawkes and the fact that, unable to stand it any longer, we had arranged to return Samson to the breeder that afternoon. We were particularly sad about that. We had grown very fond of Samson in the short time he had been with us and Samson, when he could spare the time from worrying about Solomon and Sheba, was obviously fond of us too.

We felt we had failed in our handling of the cats – and that, though she was kindness itself in saying how sorry she was and agreeing to take him back, was undoubtedly the opinion of the breeder. Her kittens, she told us when we rang her up, often went to homes where there were other cats – even other Siamese – and after the initial settling-down period there had never been any trouble with *them*. The inference was that if we had given it a little more time and been firmer with our own two specimens – though how we could have done that, short of putting them in balls and chains, we didn't know – we wouldn't have had any trouble either.

Dr Tucker soon put us right on that score. Nothing, he said, could have altered the situation. It arose from the fact that Solomon and Sheba were twins and had been brought up together. They had a much greater affinity, he said, than kittens raised together but coming from different families – and though in time they might have come to tolerate Samson it would only have been an armed truce. Never would there have been the affection that, despite their feuds and battles, our two held for each other. Never the fun, either. In due course Solomon and Sheba themselves might – as they had already begun to do – have grown completely apart. In any case, he said, glancing professionally at Solomon who all this time had been sitting in the road with the owlishly innocent expression he always adopted when people were talking about him – in any case, with Solomon so jealous and Samson being another tom, eventually Solomon would have started to spray.

Solomon's ears shot up like train signals at that and so did ours. Solomon, we said – firmly, in case the gremlins were listening – was neutered. Before he could look round, Solomon assured him soulfully – though there was a distinctly speculative look in his eye, too. We were stunned when the doctor explained to us that while neuters didn't usually go in for such pastimes there was nothing – once they were roused to jealousy over another cat and particularly, it seemed, if they were Siamese – to stop them. We were even more stunned when we realised what an escape we'd had. As Charles remarked more than once on the way home, once Solomon got the idea he wouldn't have stopped at spraying. He'd have gone round acting like a stirrup pump. All the perfumes of Arabia, said Charles, fanning himself faintly at the very thought, wouldn't have helped us in that case. One whiff and we'd have been out of bounds for weeks.

So, less reluctantly than we would otherwise have parted with him but sadly nevertheless, we took Samson back to his family. The last we saw of him he wasn't worrying about us at all but was simply a fat black paw happily baiting his sisters round a bookcase. And gradually life returned to normal.

Only gradually. It was several days before Sheba finally stopped spitting at Solomon – and Solomon, in turn, stopped going round as if he expected to see Dracula round every corner. But eventually peace did return, and with it the morning when, as soon as the door of the spare room was opened, they marched happily in to us side by side. Sheba pausing to wash Solomon's ears before she cuddled down on Charles's shoulder and Solomon, by way of his own private celebration, diving head-first under the bedclothes, rolling on his back, and going to sleep with his feet on the pillow.

Now, for the first time in weeks, we had a chance to look round and see what was happening in the village.

Things hadn't been exactly standing still there, either. Something had upset Father Adams – what it was we didn't know yet, but it was a sure sign when every time he passed the cottage he had his hat so far down over his eyes he could hardly see. The people down the lane had a new car. (Cream with a nice hard top reported Solomon, watching it with interest from the window and agitating the curtains so hard they probably thought it was us. Just the thing for autographing. He must go down and walk over it as soon as possible.) And Sidney, with Christmas looming ahead, had temporarily given up odd-jobbing and was working for a local builder. With results which, from what we could hear, were likely to set the housing programme back for years.

Sidney laughingly told us some of them when he came to mend a tap one Sunday morning. In one house, it seemed – working with a double team because it was wanted in a hurry – they'd whipped the walls up so fast it wasn't till lunch-time, when somebody went to fill the kettle, that they realised they hadn't left any gaps for the doors. There was no need to ask who'd filled them in; it was, of course, Sidney.

In another one they had for days been going in and out by means of a space left for a large plate glass observation window. Apart from filling kettles Sidney's gang apparently never used doorways in the normal way, but leapt light-heartedly through windows or over four-foot walls to show their agility. Thus it was that not ten minutes after the window *had* been put in place one bright autumn morning another member of the team, late for work on account of his motorbike breaking down, had come tearing up the path, taken off at the spot from which Sidney & Co. usually launched themselves across the sill, and before anybody could stop him had gone clean through it.

He hadn't hurt himself – head like a coconut he had, Sidney assured us; all he got was ringing in his ears and a dent in his driving helmet – and they'd laughed themselves sick over it for days. Until, in fact, their next hilarious little faux pas, when they put a staircase in backwards.

This was in a contemporary house – the first ever to go up in our village – and this time, said Sidney, knocking our stopcock for six with the coal hammer, it was the boss's fault. We were glad to hear that. We were beginning to have visions of Sidney and his pals spending Christmas in the workhouse if they went on at this rate, and it was a relief to hear of a little balance coming into their affairs.

On this occasion, it seemed, the boss couldn't understand the plans. Brought up on solid, foursquare bungalows and good old semi-detacheds, his first open-plan layout had floored him completely. Not wishing to confess it he had puzzled it out as best he could – with the result that the staircase had gone in the wrong way round and in one place passed so close under a beam they had to go on hands and knees to navigate it.

The funny thing about that, said Sidney – dealing our tap a clonk which certainly stopped it leaking, though whether it would ever run again was another matter – was that everybody did go under it on hands and knees. The boss, the workmen – even the people the house was being built for. Somehow, Sidney said, it just grew on them as part of the construction; nobody stopped to think they'd still be doing it when the house was finished. Nobody, that is, until the architect came down from London, and what *he* said when he saw them playing Oranges and Lemons up his staircase – Sidney said he turned bright purple, and it didn't come out of the dictionary.

Never believe it would we? asked Sidney, downing his hammer and looking hopefully at the teapot. We would, alas. Only too well. Back in the days when we had Blondin and had just moved into the cottage we, too, had innocently engaged a local builder to level the kitchen. After several days during which I washed up with one foot on a plank and one knee on the sink to avoid falling into six inches of cement and the builder told us unceasingly how clever he was – never used a spirit level, he assured us; never used a plumb line either; just went by his eye and never made a mistake in his life – the boards were removed to reveal that at long last, and unfortunately on our kitchen floor, myopia had caught up with him. It was still two inches out of true.

When we pointed it out to the builder, first of all he swore it wasn't and then – when we proved it by putting one of Blondin's nuts at the top and letting it roll down the slope – he said he'd done it purposely. So that when I threw a bucket of water over it it would run straight out of the back door he said, with sudden inspiration. Nothing – not even our protests that if we did the first thing it would do would be to run straight into the cupboards – would move him. And there, a monument to the invincibility of local builders, our floor slopes gently to this day. With cooker, three cabinets (and now of course the refrigerator) supported on the blocks he provided not only to level them up but presumably so we could throw water under them as well.

Not, as Charles said, that we could have told Sidney that. It might have given him ideas. Not that we had much chance to dwell on our kitchen floor, either. That was the morning Sheba got bitten by an adder.

I know it was October and that adders usually bite in the Spring. That was what the vet said when I rang him up and told him – though as an afterthought he said our cats were capable of finding anacondas in January if they felt like it and he'd better come over right away. I know it was always Solomon we'd worried about over adders. Solomon, whose idea of capturing anything from a grass snake to a wasp was to poke it first to see if it moved and then sniff it to see if it was good to eat. Solomon, who when we took him for a walk dived impressively into every clump of grass we came to and then got so excited, seeing his own black paw emerge on the other side, that if an adder had been there he would have been a trophy on its totem pole before he could look round.

Not that Sheba was a snake-catcher either. It was just that – being so good at everything – we'd always imagined that if she did go in for snaking she'd come home wearing them like leis. Which was why when she crept sadly into the cottage on three legs, holding one paw in the air and looking pitifully at us as she passed, to begin with we didn't worry too much. There was always the chance she was imitating Solomon; apart from which we'd had so many false alarms with one or other of them falling off walls, the vet rushing over to diagnose sprains, and cats' liniment at 7/6d a time simply piling up in the bathroom – unused, because they hid the moment they saw the bottle – we informed her the slings were in the first-aid cabinet and continued talking to Sidney.

It wasn't till we discovered she was under the bed and that her paw, normally so small and neat, was the size of a balloon that we realised there was something wrong – and by that time it was almost too late. When we got her out from under the bed she was already in a coma. She lay in Charles's arms as if she were dead while I phoned the vet. Completely limp she lay there – though by this time her eyes were slightly open – while he examined her, said it did indeed look like snakebite and we could take no chances, and swiftly injected histamine into her rump.

That was to stop the swelling. For the next half-hour our world stood still, while we waited to see if it acted and the vet arranged to get snake-serum, if it were needed, from the local hospital. I had her by this time – close in my arms for warmth, with Charles and Sidney standing by and Solomon, always to the forefront in a drama, peering curiously from a nearby chair.

Never had she seemed so dear to us as she lay there while the minutes passed and the swelling rose slowly to her shoulder – not even in those long night hours when she was lost. Then at least there was a chance that she was safe somewhere. Now we could only watch her and know that if she left us – wicked, destructive, maddening as she was – part of our hearts would go too.

There was, as Charles said when it was all over, no need for us to have worried. Sheba was made of tougher stuff than that. Quite apart from anything else she wasn't going to bequeath all the fish to Solomon if she could help it.

Half an hour later, with the swelling miraculously halted and Sheba herself happily playing Camille on a hot-water bottle, the vet pronounced her out of danger. All that remained now, he said, patting her gently on the cheek, was for the little girl to get better.

The little girl did that all right. After a couple of days' convalescence on our bed, with Charles carrying her up and down stairs because her foot still swelled when she walked – and the only thing she could *eat*, she assured us casting triumphant glances at Solomon every time she saw him gloomily chewing cod, was gallons and gallons of crab paste – she was as right as rain. When she did get up she nearly drove us mad for days drinking water non-stop with the noise of a St Bernard – but that, said the vet when we reported it, was just her system counteracting the effect of the histamine. After we'd opened the kitchen door for her about fifty times in an evening it seemed to us more like Sheba being cussed, but eventually, just before our legs gave out, that wore off too.

All that remained was Sheba telling everybody ad nauseam how she'd been bitten by an adder and nearly died; a certain cogitation on the part of ourselves and the vet as to whether it might, after all, have been a wasp; and a firm conviction on the part of Sheba that Sidney – when we looked back we realised that he had indeed been standing behind her at the time – was the one who stuck the hypodermic into her. Right in the Bot, she reproached him every time he appeared. Right where it Hurt. Just when she was Almost

Dying. Sidney did his best to make it up, but she wouldn't go near him for weeks.

ELEVEN

Solomon's Friend Timothy

The next thing that happened to us was Timothy. The boy with the catapult. One morning he broke our kitchen window with a deft shot round the coalhouse and while he was still gazing admiringly at the hole Charles nipped out of the back gate and grabbed him. We had been wondering for days who he belonged to. Now, when we marched him off, cowboy hat and all, to try and find who owned him, nobody was more surprised than we were when he suddenly fled howling up Father Adams's path.

He was, it seemed, the Adamses' grandson, and he was staying with them to give his mother a rest. The reason we hadn't found it out before was that we personally had been busy with our own problems over the cats; in the winter we only saw Father Adams (to talk to, anyway) at weekends; and Father Adams, when we said fancy our not knowing about a thing like that, said he believed in keeping his troubles to himself.

That I remembered as one of Grandma's favourite opening remarks, too – and sure enough next moment we were hearing the lot. The things Timothy had done at home – the last of which, nearly prostrating his mother for good and all, had been to swallow the axle off a toy motorcar. It wasn't that so much that upset her, explained Father Adams – though she did faint off a couple of times when she thought of it going round in Timothy's stomach. It was the fact that when the doctors got him to hospital and had him X-rayed they couldn't find it.

They said he hadn't swallowed it. He said he had. His mother, beside herself with worry, was expecting it to puncture his vitals at any moment. When, following a hunch, a doctor and nurse accompanied them home and said now what about the little man showing them where it was – and he, bright as a button, produced it from the table drawer – she practically had hysterics. Why, she wept, before fainting off for the third time, had he told her he'd swallowed it? Laughing happily at his little joke on Mum he said he *had*. And then he'd sicked it up.

How, in face of Timothy's record, we came to ask him to tea with us I haven't a clue. He'd not only broken our window. To date, while under the guardianship of Father Adams, he'd eaten the bus-tickets on a trip to town and caused trouble with the inspector, broken the window of the Rose and Crown (also with his catapult; he said his Granfer was inside and he wanted to speak to him, which we thought showed initiative but apparently the landlord didn't), and painted the Ferrys' gateposts a bright, Post-Office red.

The trouble there was that Fred Ferry had only recently done them pea-green. He came up the lane raving about Timothy ruining his brand-new paint with that rotten muck; Father Adams – who happened to be rather fond of red and the paint Timothy had used was in fact some left over from his own front door – took offence and offered to punch him on the nose; Fred Ferry, in typical village fashion, had now taken out a summons against him – and if he got away with it under a fiver, said Father Adams, clapping his hat despondently over his eyes at the very thought, he'd be another ruddy Dutchman.

Maybe we'd been reading the church magazine and had our haloes on just then, but ask Timothy to tea we did. Turning the other cheek and hoping, perhaps – ignoring the job we'd so far made of Solomon and Sheba – to reform him.

I regret to say that didn't work either. He drank his tea – when he didn't spill it on the carpet – with noises reminiscent of a blocked drain. The cats were absolutely *fascinated*. He ate his bread and butter with both hands, gazing stolidly at us over the top of it as if it were some sort of earthwork. In spite of our attempts at conversation he said absolutely nothing. When he had finished, in reply to our query as to what he'd like to do now, he marched over to the window, picked up ashtray, gave it a couple of taps to get its surroundings, and smashed it carefully on the sill. After that he went home – during which process Charles, hastening to open the door for him, accidentally stepped on another ashtray which we'd put on the floor for safety.

Only at the door did Timothy speak. 'The man broke he,' he announced with satisfaction.

The next move amazes me to this day. The following morning Timothy came down, swung silently on our gate for a while and then, when he found I was taking no notice of him after his behaviour at tea, took a pot shot at Solomon who was digging in the garden. He missed him. Not that that influenced me. Livid with anger, completely forgetting the church magazine, I flew out intending to give him the tanning of his life. But when I reached the gate Timothy was still standing there gazing at Solomon in complete astonishment.

'He spoke to I,' he said, quite forgetting to run in his amazement. He had indeed. As the stone whizzed past his ear, just when he was a sitting duck, Solomon had given a loud, indignant bellow. What intrigued Timothy wasn't so much his speaking – he'd been living with Mimi for a fortnight now and was used to Siamese rumination by this time. It was that he had such a deep bass voice. Why, Timothy wanted to know, was his voice different from Mimi's? Because he was a boy of course, I said. How did I know he was a boy, asked Timothy, his interest growing with every second. I had to think jolly fast about that one. Because of his voice, I said.

If anyone had said that a cat could solve the problem of Timothy I would never have believed them. Certainly not Solomon, who for four years now had been a full-time problem himself. But he did. Timothy – who had no animals at all in his home in town and didn't, it seemed, think much of girl cats like Mimi – was absolutely entranced at the thought of Solomon being a boy. Solomon in turn, having graciously forgiven Timothy for the stone, thought he was pretty good too. From then on we had a mutual admiration society around the place that nothing could shake.

In some ways it was very useful. Ever since he was a kitten one of our biggest nightmares, when we had to go to town, had been to get Solomon in beforehand. Sheba's treks to the strawberry patch had turned out to be a passing phase and, in true Siamese fashion, had indeed stopped completely as soon as the strawberry season was over and the old man didn't get mad with her any more.

Solomon, however – at any given time and particularly if we had a train to catch – could be practically depended on to be missing. Asleep in a field if it was warm; sheltering in somebody's coalhouse if it was wet (or, which was equally possible, sitting in the rain watching somebody's ducks); and if it was just ordinary, anywhere from visiting the Rector to beating it rapidly up the valley.

When I called him he came eventually. With Solomon, however, eventually could be anything from five minutes for a final sniff at a daisy to two hours during which I tore madly round the lanes in town clothes and gumboots wondering if my job was still open. It was wonderful, after the advent of Timothy, to be able either to open the door and spot them at once or else – if it was early and Timothy wasn't around yet – to call him out, get him to do his two-fingered whistle, and watch while Solomon, with his latest Trigger-friend-of-Man expression on his face, appeared at the speed of Alice's Cheshire.

It cost us a considerable amount in chocolate. Timothy, reformed or not, wasn't the boy to do things for love alone. At times, with the church magazine far behind us, we even had a sneaking suspicion that it wasn't so much a case of Solomon vanishing and Timothy finding him but of Solomon staying where he was told while Timothy collected the reward.

There was also a slight disadvantage in that Timothy now insisted on coming with us on walks. We and the cats were bad enough. We, the cats and a small boy in a cowboy hat who every now and then gave an ear-splitting whistle – whereupon one large Seal Point bounced excitedly to heel and one small Blue Point immediately sat down and said she wasn't coming any further – were slightly *outré* even for our village.

We couldn't have everything, however. And at least Timothy had put away his catapult and was taking an interest in nature. He took such an interest in it that eventually Charles, after a particularly embarrassing conversation about cows right outside the Rector's gate, refused to come with us any more. I was better suited to deal with such questions than he was, he said. So he and Sheba, cowards that they were, stayed at home working on the kitchen. Which was why, the day we saw the rabbit, Timothy, Solomon and I were on our own.

It was frightfully exciting for us naturalists. I hadn't seen a rabbit since myxomatosis. Solomon had never seen one at all and immediately went up a tree in case it was a wolf. Timothy, who had heard about them but had never seen one in his life either, wanted to know all about it. An excellent little lecture I gave on rabbits and their habits. At the end of which Timothy announced that he wanted to spend a penny.

Chastened – for it seemed he hadn't been listening at all – but thankful nevertheless that for once we were in the woods and not where he usually felt like it, which was bang in the middle of the village, I discreetly turned my back. There was a slight pause. 'Going now,' said Timothy, quite unnecessarily. 'Down a rabbit hole,' he announced a moment later. And then – to Solomon, loudly, and obviously pondering my story after all – 'Rabbits'll think it's raining, won't they?' he said solemnly.

They made admirable foils for each other, Timothy and Solomon. One moment so wistful – like the time Timothy, gazing round-eyed up at the craggy hill behind us, said if they fell off there they'd be dead wouldn't they and go to heaven, and never eat any tea again ever 'cos they'd only be bones – whereupon I blew my nose hastily and the Rector's wife went straight out and bought him three boxes of caps for his pistol. The next so aggravating – like the time I found him standing on his head on our stairs, walking complicatedly up and down the wall in his gumboots while Solomon sat proudly by like a ringmaster – I could have spanked the pair of them.

Everybody admired the picture they made together. Everybody, that is, except Sheba, who went round them in a wide semicircle when she met them in the lane, assured everybody she met that she didn't know them at all, and forecast darkly to us when she came in that before long Solomon would be using a catapult too and the pair of them would end up behind bars. Everybody – even Father Adams – said how it had improved Timothy. Darn he if he wouldn't get 'un a kitten for hisself when he went home, he said – whereupon Sheba squawked her approval and immediately offered him Sol.

What was worrying us was how Solomon would react when Timothy did go back to town. Animals, they say, form strange attachments for children. Only recently we had heard of a Siamese called Augustus who had been an absolute terror in his original home. Shouting, stealing, fighting cats and intimidating dogs – in the end they'd had to practically give him away to get him adopted at all. In his new home, however, they had a little girl, with whom Augustus had fallen in love so completely that when she went into hospital to have her tonsils out it wasn't she her parents worried about but Augustus, who went into a decline on her bed, said his heart was broken, refused to get up or eat, and pretty nearly died. In the end, for his sake, they had to get her home from hospital at the first possible moment and let her convalesce in bed – where, we gathered, she and Augustus ate ice cream and arrowroot together, eventually got up together, and when last heard of were living very happily indeed.

It wouldn't be like that for Solomon. Even if Father Adams's summons went off all right Timothy wouldn't be back at least until the Spring. How, we wondered, would our black man manage when he went away?

As it happened, very well indeed. Solomon did wait by the gate for him the first morning – until he spotted me in the greenhouse trying to let out a blue tit which had flown in and was trapped. He soon forgot Timothy in the excitement of trying to help me catch it – and of being bundled, yelling his head off, indoors, where he sat in the window roaring furiously about not being allowed to be a Sportsman.

I thought he looked pathetic the next morning, too, hunched motionless on the garden wall with Sheba – out

TWELVE

Highly Entertaining

The cats didn't like the winter. Sheba, who had rather a thin coat, complained because it was cold. The first sign of a frost in our house was indeed not the pipes bursting or the dahlias turning black but Sheba sitting hopefully in front of electric fires waiting for them to be switched on. Solomon, on the other hand, having a coat like a beaver, a circulation that was apparently oil-fired and an insatiable desire to be out, complained because he was kept in.

He was kept in – comparatively speaking, that is, as against his ranging freedom of the summer – for three reasons. Firstly that cold, wet weather was supposed to be bad for Siamese and, as Father Adams said the day he saw him sitting on the wall watching the pigs, if we didn't watch out he'd get a chill in his backside. Secondly that after an hour

117

or so with the back door open and the east wind cutting through like a knife Charles would suggest that we got him in and shut it before we got a chill in ours. And thirdly that it wasn't safe for him to be out after dark on account of foxes and badgers.

It was the last part that annoyed him most. Darkness, with the foxes barking in the woods and the sound of badgers grunting their way up the track to their playground in the clearing on the hillside, was just when Solomon wanted to be out.

Every night after supper he would make a tour of the windows. Hear that? he would demand, sticking his head indignantly through the curtains as a mournful hooting came from up in the oak tree. Owls. People let *them* out. Hear that? he would wail as a vixen called way off in the darkness. Foxes. Nobody kept them in. Hear that? he would entreat as the sound of cracking branches told of animals with white striped snouts lumbering clumsily through the undergrowth. Badgers. Supposed we never wanted him to *see* a badger, he would complain, his voice rising to an aggrieved wail. Knowing his propensity for poking things with his paw and, as Charles said, not wanting a cat with a wooden leg around the place, he was certainly right there.

What with outbursts like this from him and Sheba eternally complaining that her Ears were Freezing (they were too; like most Blue Points they had hardly any fur on them at all, five feet from the fire and you could practically see the icicles) our cats certainly didn't like the winter. Neither did the Rector's, who marched indignantly indoors with the first frost, announced that they were half Siamese and this was when it showed, and promptly went to earth under the eiderdown.

Neither, if it came to that, did the Rector. The electricity supply wasn't too good at our end of the village. This was the time of year when he was faced with the tricky little problem that if he switched on the heating in the church the villagers complained because their lights went down, and if he didn't the organist complained because the damp made the keys stick on the organ – when, passing his study window, he could be seen with a decidedly unecclesiastic expression on his face writing to the Electricity Board.

We liked the winter. Hope, as several people said when they heard about our adopting Samson, certainly sprang eternal in our breasts – and never did it spring more strongly than when winter came upon us. When, after a long and arduous summer we looked forward to a period of rest. Dormant, as Charles poetically put it, as the season itself. Reading our books. Relaxing by the fire. Entertaining our friends.

The fact that it never turned out like that – that the long and arduous summer was invariably followed by a longer and even more arduous winter – meant nothing to us. This year, we told ourselves annually, was going to be different.

This year, as a matter of fact, Solomon opened the proceedings the day the clocks went back by swallowing a prawn's head. Celebrating the beginning of the season in our own quiet manner, we had invited friends round to supper. Making sure Solomon was well out of the way – he was, to be exact, sitting on a notice board up on the hillside; a notice board which was there to stop people going up a private road but which, since he had adopted it as his personal crow's nest, now leaned so far forward nobody could read what it said – I was shelling prawns for scampi.

The wind was in my favour, Solomon I thought was scanning the horizon for Sheba – that, of course, was where I made my mistake. Solomon was actually scanning it for prawns. I left my post for just two seconds to check that the table was properly set, and by the time I got back there he was going backwards round the kitchen with one jammed firmly in his throat and that was the end of relaxation for *that* evening.

Supper was late, our guests arrived just in time to help hold him down while the vet got it out, and hardly was that little crisis safely over than Solomon was sick. Not on account of the prawn but as a reminiscent afterthought, halfway through the coffee.

Solomon was often sick when people came. Not because he felt ill. It just happened that when we had visitors his favourite place was on the bureau, keeping an Oriental eye on them. After a while, when nothing exciting happened like somebody eating something or somebody wanting a game with his Ping-Pong ball, he would get bored and yawn. When he yawned, being Solomon, he did it in style. A great big noisy yawn about a foot wide that invariably over-reached itself – and there he was. Sick. Usually down the front of the bureau, where he sat and watched entranced while it trickled round the carving and looked most hurt when people moved away.

When he wasn't sick, Sheba quite often bit her nails for us. When we were spared that, Solomon could be depended on to want his earth box. In the spare room it was. Out of sight but not, unfortunately, of sound. However loudly we talked – and crescendo had nothing on us when we saw him disappearing into the hall – there was always somebody to peer at the ceiling a moment later and ask what on earth *that* noise was. Always somebody, too, to say 'Niagara Falls'.

Not, mind you, that the cats were responsible for everything that happened to us on social occasions. The time Charles fell through a chair, for instance, in somebody else's house – we could hardly blame them for that. We could hardly blame our hosts, either. All they said by way of friendly conversation was that they had picked it up at a sale last week for ten bob, and didn't we think it was a bargain. It was a shock to them, too, when Charles, who was sitting in it, seized the arms, braced himself rigidly against the back to test it – and before anybody could do anything about it, there was a sudden crack and the seat collapsed.

Neither was it the cats' fault the night the same people came to visit us back and Charles offered them gin and lime.

They were quite happy with gin and tonic. We hadn't touched lime juice ourselves for months – not since the day I spilt some on a table and it took all the polish off, and Charles got worried about its effect on his stomach. Why he offered it right then I couldn't imagine, but unfortunately he did.

Unfortunately, because when he went out to the kitchen and found that what we did have had gone peculiar he didn't leave it at that and say we'd run out. He brought it in to show them. Sorry chaps but it was a bit high, he said, waving before their astonished eyes a bottle absolutely covered in dust and containing what looked like a flotilla of long-dead fish. Would they perhaps rather go without?

Not only that but, covertly eyeing the remains of their gins and tonics to make sure there weren't any peculiar things in *them*, it wasn't long before they went home as well.

Things like that happen to everybody at times, of course. A neighbour of ours was making ham croquettes one night for her visitors and got the mincer stuck, and when she called her husband and he couldn't unjam it he threw it out through the door. Because he was naturally mad with it and, according to him, because he thought the jolt might loosen it. What in fact did happen was that the mincer pitched in a bed of stinging nettles, they couldn't get it out without cutting the whole lot down and there wasn't time for that, so she had to rush up and borrow ours. Did things ever go wrong like that for us? she asked tearfully as I hauled it out of the cupboard and blew the cobwebs off. Almost every day, I assured her.

With us, as a matter of fact, things could go wrong even when we were *not* having visitors. Not having them, that is, in the sense of trying to put them off. Most people do that at some time or other – on account of being tired, or having booked up two lots of people by mistake, or, when the time comes deciding that they just can't face up to it.

That was what happened with the Joneses. Charles himself had invited them round for the evening. Charles himself, every time I groaned at the thought, kept saying we had to ask them some time and if we played cards or something it wouldn't be too bad. And it was Charles himself who, the day they were due to come, had a vision halfway through tea of old Jones being hearty and bellowing the place down like a foghorn and Mrs Jones being coy and wanting to play whist, and said he couldn't stand it. Not today, he said. Next week perhaps – but not today. He wasn't feeling strong enough. Couldn't I ring up and say he was dead?

What I did say, going hot and cold all over and quite certain they knew I was cramming, was that I thought he had a cold. An excuse that has probably been used a million times before – but I bet this was the only time it was greeted at the other end by the assurance that they didn't mind a bit; never caught colds; hadn't had one for years; what old Charles wanted was somebody to cheer him up and not to worry, they were coming right on over.

That put us on the spot all right. There was Charles saying his reputation was ruined. There was I – after all, I was the one who'd made the excuse – thinking mine was too. There was the clock ticking on to seven-thirty. When suddenly I had an idea. In the circumstances it was a jolly good one, too. All it involved was Charles taking a really sound pinch of snuff.

It worked all right, though I had to stand over him to see he did it thoroughly. By the time the Joneses came – throwing wide the windows, slapping him on the back and simply dying, they said, for a nice game of whist – he was sneezing so hard he wasn't worrying about his reputation. All he was worrying about was whether he'd ruined his nose.

Winter pursued quite a moderate course after that. Nothing untoward happened at all that I can remember. Friends came and went, and played canasta with the cats sitting on their laps, and talked of world affairs. The only thing of note at all was the night somebody went into the bathroom and tugged and tugged, and just as it got to the stage (owing to the acoustics you can, unfortunately, hear the tugging all over the cottage) where we usually yell through the door to give one good pull and *wait*, then it'll work – just as we reached that stage the door of the sitting room opened and in came the visitor, rather red in the face, clutching the chain. Come off in her hand, she said it had – but it wasn't exactly surprising. Mighty tough was our flush. People'd been tolling it like a bell for years.

Nothing unusual, in fact, had happened for ages – until the night we went to see Charles's friend Allister, and Allister got Charles interested in Yoga. Allister is always getting Charles interested in something. Once, when Solomon and Sheba were small, it was archery and they nearly winged the kittens. Once it was the proposition for removing rock from behind the cottage with dynamite. Fortunately for the cottage the proposition fell through. Now – unfortunately for me – it was Yoga.

Allister hadn't done any himself. So far he'd only read a book about it. A jolly interesting book, as he said, and when I heard his description I was quite keen to read it myself. I wasn't at all surprised when Charles said he was going to get it from the library. What did alarm me – knowing from experience what Charles's enthusiasm could mean – was when, after several sessions of intense study, he announced that he was taking it up.

I spoke to Grandma, who had a lot of influence with Charles, about that. But all *she* did, after listening to him intently with her spectacles on the end of her nose, was encourage him. Most interesting she said it was, and there was a great deal in some of these things. Charles might learn much from it. If she were younger she would take up Yoga too.

Well, there we were. Charles meditating all over the place with Grandma's blessing and practising deep breathing. The cats sitting importantly by him meditating as well and announcing that they used to do this in Siam. Any minute now I expected to see the three of them wearing turbans. Until, once again, I had an idea.

This, like the snuff one, was also born of desperation. We were visiting some friends who lived on the moors at the time – staying with them, as the weather was bad, for the night. It was winter still, of course, and all the evening Charles had been talking happily of Yoga – how it mentally lifted one… raised one above bodily things… he didn't, he announced (wonderful indeed, seeing there were several degrees of frost) even feel the cold.

I did. When we went to bed – without bottles because we'd been talking so late and Charles said we really didn't need them, not feeling the cold – I was absolutely perished. Round about two o'clock in the morning I got out and put the floor-rugs on the bed, but it made no difference. I was still perished.

Charles, who had rolled over while I was getting the rugs and was now comfortably cocooned in at least three-quarters of the bedclothes, informed me once more that he didn't feel the cold. Mind over matter, he assured me, snuggling cosily into his pillow. I ought to take up Yoga. I ought to meditate too.

I did. After a little meditation I put my hand on one of the bedposts – one of those old-fashioned brass ones it was – until it was icily cold. Lovingly I burrowed through the cocoon with it in search of Charles. Tenderly I placed it

THIRTEEN

With Solder and Crowbar

That was the winter Grandma's parrot Laura died. As a result, according to Grandma, of the coalman looking at her through the window.

Everybody else said it was old age. To the family's knowledge Grandma had had Laura for thirty years, and she hadn't been first-hand even then. Grandma had bought her from a pub in the belief that parrots from licensed premises (or, she said, from a sailor if you could get one) talked – and had kept her, when she turned out to be completely dumb except for screaming like a maniac at mealtimes, on the grounds that it was wicked to keep birds in such places and she couldn't send her back.

So, after a little financial adjustment (Grandma, as she told the landlord herself, was no fool) Laura had lived with her happily for thirty years. Until, in recent months, she had begun to droop, and lose her feathers, and develop a wheezy little cough. When we reminded Grandma of that, and how for weeks now Aunt Louisa had been putting whisky in her drinking water and tying a hot-water bottle to her cage every night and still Laura had gone on failing, Grandma said it was rubbish. Laura always got bronchitis in the winter, she said; Louisa always put whisky in her drinking water (a statement which we had to clarify when there were strangers present for the sake of Aunt Louisa's reputation) and it was no use our arguing. With her own eyes she had seen the coalman looking through the window with his great black face, it had frightened poor Laura, and now she was dead.

She was indeed, and there wasn't much we could do about it except change the coalman the following week and offer to get her another parrot. After which – the management of Grandma being rather wearing at times – Charles and I went down with flu.

It wasn't so bad to begin with, when only Charles had it. True it was unfortunate that the first day he took to his bed I had to go to town. When I got back the cats, whom I had left sitting happily on his chest enjoying his temperature – the first time, Sheba announced, that she had been really warm this winter – were waiting anxiously for me in the hall window. Charles hadn't fed them, complained Solomon, regarding me indignantly through the glass. Charles was groaning, said Sheba, and they'd had to come downstairs because they couldn't stand it. Charles hadn't let them Out, roared Solomon, whose idea of anybody staying home, even with double pneumonia, was to let him in and out of doors all day long. Charles was hardly a little ray of sunshine either. When I went up to see him all he said – presumably in case it helped at the inquest – was that he'd taken his temperature at three o'clock and it was a hundred and two.

For three days he lay there wilting heroically. With his knees up most of the time because Sheba had decided that *in* the bed, in a little cave under Charles's knees if he would kindly raise them for her, was the warmest place to be. Calling feebly for more food – not because he was hungry but because by the time he'd braced himself to tackle his soup or his poached plaice Solomon, who didn't believe in this weaker brethren business, had appreciatively eaten the lot. Assuring me, when I asked how he was, that he felt very frail indeed… very frail.

It was on Monday, however, when Charles was on the convalescent list and I had taken to my bed, that the fun really started. Not that it was exactly fun for me. I had a temperature too, and to my poor, flu-befuddled mind it seemed more like one of those symbolic plays where people keep walking in and out.

First it was the cats, coming in with round, astonished eyes to ask what on earth I was doing there and when was I going to get up. Lying there instead of Charles, said Sheba reproachfully, and I *knew* she liked it under his knees. Then it was Charles, asking if he should make a cup of tea. Then, a few minutes later, it was the cats again – Charles having apparently decided there wasn't much chance of my making it, anyway – appearing to report that he wasn't half mucking about in the kitchen and he hadn't given them their breakfast yet. Then it was Solomon, howling wrathfully downstairs, charging – grumbling loudly to himself – up to his earth box in the spare room, and then appearing dramatically in the doorway once more to inform me (even in bed I was still in charge in Solomon's little world) that Charles hadn't changed it, Charles wouldn't let him out, and if I didn't do something quick there'd be an accident.

At that point I summoned strength to yell for Charles, whereupon the cats were let out, I got my cup of tea, Charles – flushed with achievement – announced that he would now get the breakfast, and, save for a monotonous creak… BANG from down below where the sitting-room door latched itself firmly every time he went through (and what on earth he was *doing* going through it about fifty times a minute I couldn't imagine) there was peace.

It lasted about five minutes, at the end of which Charles called up to say the post van hadn't arrived yet and ought he to get Solomon in – after which my next diversion was Charles in the garden calling Solomon. Shortly after that there was the sound of a tray being deposited on the hall table. Breakfast now, I told myself, and felt quite hungry at the thought. But no. Charles, having got it that far, was once more in the garden calling Solomon…

It took twenty minutes to round up Solomon and get that tray up to my bed. By that time the toast was stone-cold – which Charles said was odd, because it was hot enough when he made it. The tea was cold too. Colder even than the toast. Understandably so when I questioned Charles and found that he hadn't made a fresh pot. Having, he said, only poured one cup each out of it, and there was still bags left, he'd used the lot he'd made an hour ago.

I will skim the details of the rest of the morning, taken up by the Rector arriving to enquire whether he could get us anything in town (yes, I replied gratefully via Charles; a rabbit for the cats); Charles coming up again to ask what *size* rabbit; Charles shouting at me from the garden could I see, because the Rector was waving to me from the road; Charles coming up ten minutes later to ask whether I was awake and should he make some coffee; and, ever and anon, the cats marching in like a Greek chorus to enquire was I *still* in bed, they didn't like what Charles had given them for breakfast, and – once again – Charles wouldn't let them out.

By then it was lunch-time. There was no need for Charles to ask me what he should do about that. Before he wore his legs out completely I got up and fixed it myself.

What followed was, of course, inevitable. After all that work Charles had a relapse. By afternoon he was back in bed and I was tottering up with cups of tea for him. By evening, too – and there was no denying it; Sidney said he could hear him from the other end of the garden – Charles had a cough. There was no need – as Sheba said, snug once more in her little tent under Charles's knees while Solomon lay determinedly on his chest, heaving like a storm-tossed sailor with every wheeze – to ask who was most sick in this house. It was undoubtedly Charles.

He recovered eventually, of course. By the end of the week, with people going down like flies all over the village and the cats sitting on the wall happily informing people as they passed that we'd had it first, Charles – except for his cough – was quite flourishing. Which was how, looking round for something to occupy us during convalescence, we came to re-string the grandfather clock.

You remember, perhaps, the grandfather clock. The one in the hall, where Sheba used to sit on top and Solomon was eternally opening the door to watch it tick? We'd found a key for it eventually, and for a while there'd been peace. Sheba had even given up sitting on the top. No fun in that, she said, if old Podgebelly wasn't mucking about underneath.

And then one day the key broke off in the lock, and we were back where we started. Sheba sitting on the top, Solomon hanging through the door, entrancedly watching the pendulum. He was taller now than he had been – or else a bit more athletic. And when we went home one night and, when I opened the hall door, only Solomon ambled through, I had the fright of my life. No sign of Sheba, the door of the clock wide open, and – the silence struck me immediately – no sound of ticking from the clock...

I hardly dared look, so sure I was of what I'd find. Sheba lying in the bottom of the clock flat as a pancake, with a weight on top of her – pushed in experimentally by Solomon or, as she was apt to do when nobody was about, having an inquisitive look on her own account and over-balancing.

Sheba, as it happened, was asleep on our bed. Frozen to the eiderdown, she said when I found her there a few minutes later and hugged her with relief. Which was why she hadn't come down, and I'd be a lot more useful if I got her a hot-water bottle. Solomon it was who'd stopped the clock. Want to see how? he enquired excitedly as I set it going again. Standing on his thin hind legs he opened the door, reached in a long black paw and prodded the pendulum. Clever, wasn't he? he said.

After that little scare we went back to tying the door with string while we were away, and it was just as well we did. One night we went home to find that the clock had stopped again – and this time, when we opened the door to find out why, one of the weights *was* off. The catgut had snapped and it was lying in the bottom.

So, during our convalescence, it seemed an apt time to re-hang it. Quietly, contemplatively – with, as Charles said, plenty of time to appreciate the way craftsmen of old did their work.

What the craftsmen of old did with grandfather clocks, as we discovered when we started in on ours, was to hang the weights on catgut, tie the ends in knots inside a couple of hollow cogwheels – and then bung the clock face on fast, right in front of the cogwheels and fixed so firmly that we couldn't get it off.

We used everything but a crowbar on it before we'd finished, and still we couldn't get it off. We never did get it off. We were in fact fast reaching the stage of jumping on it when Father Adams looked in to see how we were and informed us that you didn't put new gut in like that. Not by taking off the hands and strewing pendulum, weights and pieces of clock case all over the floor. You eased it – with a piece of wire if necessary, but definitely without touching the clock face – in through they little holes. . .

We managed it in the end. What Charles said before we'd finished about the craftsmen of old and those little holes must have scorched their ears even at a distance of a hundred-and-twenty years – but we did it. We even got the clock back together again, mounted on its pinnacle, and working. We have never, to this day, been able to replace the second hand. It got a bit bent when we were taking it off and, though we straightened it again with a hammer, every time we put it back it gets hooked up in the other hands and the clock immediately stops. For days, too, we nearly went mad because no matter what we did to it the clock kept striking on the half-hour – five at half-past four, for instance, and midnight at half-past eleven. Which, even in a household like ours, was a little muddling.

We discovered what it was eventually. We had the minute hand on upside-down. A discovery that so delighted us we forgot the vicissitudes we'd gone through to get one simple weight running on one simple piece of catgut and went round boasting of our prowess in mending clocks. Which was why, when Grandma broke the hand on her alarm clock a week or two later, she asked us, as experts, to put it right.

What we did to our own clock was, as Charles remarked only the other day, nothing to what we did to Grandma's. Quite by accident, of course. The clock had no glass in it to begin with – that had got broken one morning when the clock went off too early for Grandma's liking and she had swept it on to the floor. The hand had snapped off another morning when she put the clock under the bedclothes to muffle it and it caught in the blankets. All it needed, as Charles assured her, was a touch of solder and it would be as good as new.

The trouble there was that we weren't very expert with solder. At least four times we got the hand on – success at last! said Charles each time we did it – only to find we'd soldered it to the other one and they both went round together. And when at last we did get it on by itself we discovered that during our endeavours the clock face – the little circle round the hands – had been badly scorched by the soldering iron.

We painted that – or rather Charles did, being the artist of the family – with aluminium paint. Which made the rest of the clock face look shabby, so he painted that green. Only to discover that, in his enthusiasm, he'd painted over the numbers – so when the green paint was dry he put those in again in red. At which stage, putting in the figure twelve, he unfortunately touched the minute hand with his brush and, being very lightly soldered, it fell off again. And by the time we'd soldered it on once more the aluminium-painted circle behind it was not only scorched. The heat had cracked the paint…

Charles was for starting all over again, but I was feeling slightly cracked myself by that time. We gave it back to Grandma as it was. The hand, as I pointed out before she had a chance to say anything, was at any rate *on*.

Actually Grandma was too stunned to pass much comment. Yes, she said, gazing disbelievingly at her chameleon-like alarm clock, it was.

FOURTEEN

Right up the Pole

Spring arrived in the valley at the end of March. It needed experts to detect it, mind you. Charles still had a cough. Sidney still clung firmly to his muffler. Father Adams still clumped past the cottage every morning in a balaclava that made him deafer than ever – to protect, as we heard him informing the Rector at the top of the hill one day, his lug'oles from the frost.

But the cats knew it had come. Only a week before we had had snow, and it had been the easiest thing in the world to find them in the mornings. A small, neat line of tracks leading straight from the back door to the nearest cloche – that was Sheba. Ears down, coat stuck up like a parka, a quick dig in the early peas and in again.

A trail that wound deeply through the wastes like a traveller lost in the Antarctic – pausing to inspect a bush, digressing to look in the greenhouse, ambling haphazardly up the drive and ending at a frozen puddle – that, on the other hand, was Solomon. Sitting interestedly on the ice and listening to it crack.

We had, when we got them in again, had the usual protest meeting over the bird table – with, outside, little wrens and blue tits gratefully fluttering in the snow, and, inside, Solomon and Sheba shouting battle songs in the window. We had also witnessed an incident which Charles said sometimes came to nature-lovers like us, as a reward for diligence and patience.

One morning the cats, in the middle of raucous advice to the birds as to what they'd do if *they* laid hands on them – and it wouldn't, bawled Solomon, with his eye on his old enemy the blackbird, include giving him bacon rind, either – had suddenly gone quiet. Going in to see what was wrong, on the principle that silence in a Siamese household always means trouble – there, sure enough, was Sheba hiding behind the curtain, Solomon visible only as two ears stuck periscope-fashion above the windowsill, and magpies staging a raid outside.

Back and forwards they were going, the great black-and-white wings flashing so fast between the bird table and the woods that, as Solomon said in a small, un-Solomon-like voice from beneath the sill, there must be hundreds of them out there, and it was a jolly good thing we were in. As a matter of fact, which was the interesting thing about it, there were only two. Working, according to Charles who understands these things, to a plan of Time and Motion.

One chasing off the other birds and piling the cake over by the gate and the other – the girl she bet, said Sheba from behind her curtain; it was always the girls who did the work and the other one looked a lazypants to her, like Solomon – busily transporting it from the gate into the woods.

But now, quite suddenly, it was Spring. With Sheba sitting on the cottage roof and refusing to come down – she could, she said, see every mouse-hole for miles around and the air was fine up here – Solomon chasing a ginger tom, and Timothy arriving for the Easter holidays.

We weren't quite out of the woods yet, mind you. That night, looking for two little cats who had elected to stay out Both Ends of the Day now that Spring was here, we met the ginger tom chasing Solomon. While Timothy – presumably to keep his lug'holes warm, too – was now wearing a crash helmet.

It added, as Charles remarked, little to the decor of the cottage or to Timothy, but he refused to take it off. He also, having once renewed his acquaintance with Solomon and with us, hardly ever seemed to go home. We had Sheba on the wall busily informing people he Wasn't Ours, Solomon stalking admiringly after him being a space cat, Timothy himself performing landings on the lawn from Mars... Wunnerful how the little chap'd took to us, wasn't it? said Father Adams, beaming benignly over the gate at the mêlée on his way to the Rose and Crown – which was all very well for him.

People didn't tell him *his* little boy's trousers were coming down. People didn't tell him *his* little boy was calling them rude names in the lane, or encouraging a cat with a long black face to walk deliberately over their cars. People didn't tell him they thought that helmet was bad for *his* little boy's ears – to be met by the little boy retching realistically and sticking out his tongue. Everybody thought he was ours.

It wouldn't have been so bad if he appreciated the relationship, but he didn't. He followed Charles around informing him scathingly that he couldn't grow cabbages like his Granfer. Me he advised professionally that my rake was no good. Break he I would if Charlie-boy didn't put a nail in h'n, he said. And when a little later the rake did indeed come off the handle and I tried to slink nonchalantly past with it hidden in a bucket – did Timothy avert his gaze and ignore it like a gentleman? Like heck he did. Told I, didn't he? he said.

His one saving grace was his interest in nature, and even that had complications. Because when I pointed out the birds to him, and Charles told him about them making their nests – and then Charles, in an unguarded moment, told him of the collection of birds' eggs he had had as a boy – we had fresh problems with Timothy. He wanted a collection, too.

In vain I tried to persuade him against it. All he said, while Charles looked suitably guilty, was that Charlie-boy did. The best I could do, as the die was cast, was to stipulate sternly that he must never damage a nest, never frighten the bird, never take more than one egg – and then only if there were at least three there already. And only, in any case, I said firmly, if he was going to be a Naturalist.

He was, he assured us. On a business basis, apparently, because next time I asked after his collection he said he had six hedge sparrow's eggs already. Only one from each nest, he assured me as I clutched my head and groaned. But there were lots of them about, 'n' if he swapped one with somebody who had, say, a spare moorhen's egg, that would save him disturbing a moorhen, wouldn't it?

It would also, I hoped, giving the scheme my dubious blessing, stop Timothy from falling in the pond – which was something Charles, nostalgically remembering his own childhood, hadn't thought of.

As it was, spurred on by a book on birds which he'd persuaded Father Adams to buy for him, the next development was that Timothy started borrowing our stepladder to look at nests he'd spotted up the lane or in the woods, which meant that Charles or I – accompanied, of course, by Solomon; and, in the far, reproachful distance, Sheba – had to go with him to hold the ladder and prevent him breaking his neck.

That in itself wasn't too bad. It was all quite local – concentrated round a corner of the village where everybody thought we were nuts anyway. But one day Timothy turned up in a state of great excitement announcing that he'd found a hawfinch's nest. Over by the church, he said it was; in a rather tall hawthorn, which meant taking the ladder – and, as the branches were prickly, please could he borrow the shears?

We all went on that expedition. I got roped in – hawthorns being rather tricky – to help hold the ladder. I didn't mind that so much, but I did experience a qualm when we reached the church to find that Timothy had told us a little lie. That it wasn't, he explained, *quite* right here after all, but some way down the lane.

I guessed what lay ahead of me, and I was right. A procession down the road with me trying to look as if I always went for walks carrying the rear ends of ladders. Timothy wearing his crash helmet. The cats marching happily behind. People, as I pointed out, were looking at us even then – but it was no good telling Charles. He, re-living the halcyon days of youth, was a Naturalist too by this time. 'Take no notice,' he said.

So there – when we reached the tree and my final fears were realised; it was not in some corner of a hidden copse but hanging right over the road – I stood. Holding the ladder while Charles pruned out the branches, Timothy directed operations from the sideline, and the cats sat conspicuously on top.

Just about everybody passed us while we were there. The doctor laughing his head off, old ladies raising their eyebrows, Sidney tapping his head. What they'd be saying about us in the village I could just imagine, but it didn't worry Charles. Not, that was, until he came down out of the tree – there was nothing in the nest and it was, once more, a hedge-sparrow's – and heard what Timothy had to say. He'd just remembered, he announced. Rector'd given he a talking-to yesterday about birds'-nesting. Did we think we should go back across the fields with the ladder – so nobody'd know we'd been? he said.

Spring, in spite of that little setback, still surged steadfastly on. Starlings started nesting in the eaves and Solomon, trying to climb a wall to see them, fell down and hurt his foot. I made some dandelion wine, which attracted all the ants in the neighbourhood who immediately started getting drunk in the greenhouse. The Rector's cats got spring eczema and were going round self-consciously painted with Gentian Violet – which scared our two practically out of their points when they saw them. They thought it was Woad, they said.

We started going for walks after supper – round the village in the soft spring evenings, with the cats greeting people they hadn't seen all winter Most Friendlily and people gazing apprehensively back. We went off for a few days by the sea to get our strength up for the summer – and when Solomon's basket fell off its handle as we carried him into Halstock, there again was another sign. Woodworm on spring manoeuvres in the cover; the only part Solomon had left intact.

And finally – the one thing we needed to convince us that Spring was really with us – Tarzan the tortoise came back.

He appeared one day as magically as he had vanished, ambling down the garden helped by two excited paws. He didn't half look thin to him, said Solomon, lying down when we appeared and squinting anxiously under his shell. What about giving him some rabbit? Found him in the garage, said Sheba, beaming proudly at Charles. Under that straw heap she'd been watching for days, and wasn't she clever?

She was indeed. So was Charles, whose idea it subsequently was to paint a bull's-eye on Tarzan's back to match the cottage. White for the walls, he chanted, describing a neat lime-wash circle on his drab brown shell. Blue for the doors, he said, putting a small circle inside the first one while Timothy and the cats stood admiringly by. Now, he announced, we could *never* lose Tarzan. We could spot him anywhere he went. Even if he got out and wandered round the village, people would know he was ours.

Which was how, quite simply, we arrived at the next stage of our springtime saga. Visitors to the valley were apt to be surprised these days anyway, when at the top they met Hardy and Willis sporting purple whiskers. When, rounding the corner one morning, one of them then encountered Timothy in his crash helmet, a tortoise painted blue and white, Solomon – because at that moment Tarzan had stopped for a rest – looking worriedly underneath and Sheba, following them at a distance shouting that they were all very silly and had Better Come Right Back Home... he jumped, and turned quite pale.

That, said the villager with him, was the lot from *Cats In The Belfry*. The visitor mopped his brow. If he asked him, he said shakenly, we were ruddy well up the pole.

FIFTEEN

Cats in May

It is Maytime now in the valley. The birds are singing; the lilac is in bloom; Solomon and Sheba are moulting; and – judging by the ants in the greenhouse – our dandelion wine is a riot.

Timothy is still with us. Father Adams never got Fred Ferry's summons after all. At the eleventh hour they united instead over a right of way running through some building land. Fred Ferry says he remembers distinctly using it when he were courting... Father Adams says so does he, and the elm tree is up there still... From the sentimental expressions they assume when they are talking about it I have a strong suspicion they are making it up, particularly since if they are successful it will result, according to Father Adams, in something unique even in this district – a footpath going through a house. Meanwhile, there being nothing like a good fight for his rights to put him in a good humour, he has arranged to keep Timothy for the summer. Do 'un a power of good, he explained when he broke the news to us, and he weren't much trouble, were he?

We are resting now from the turmoil on the lawn. Charles has just come back from a hayfield, where he has spent two hours looking for Timothy's scout knife which he – Timothy, that is – and Solomon lost while they were being naturalists. Tossing it up they were, wept Timothy, when a jackdaw distracted their attention, and when they looked round it was gone.

I, as a further mark of Timothy's zest to be a naturalist, am now a swallow's Mum. One just a few days old which he found lying in the lane one night in the shelter of the barn and brought to me for succour. Much good did it do me, too, to say I didn't know what to feed it on. 'Flies caught on the wing,' advised Timothy pontifically, without a thought of the sight which would have ensued had we taken his advice. Charles and I and the cats, catching swallow's flies on the lawn.

It is, as a matter of fact, doing very nicely on boiled egg and biscuit crumbs. Fed every hour, of course, which means my taking it to town during the day, but what is that to Timothy? Or to my colleagues, to whose delight – with happy memories of Blondin – it feeds clinging to the front of my dress, looking open-beaked up at my mouth and taking egg from a matchstick with aplomb.

It lives, when we are home, in the bathroom – which is why Sheba is now sitting on the bathroom windowsill, imploring us piteously to open up. Thirsty she says she is, bawling so hard that already the Rector's wife has stopped to ask if she is Well. So thirsty she can hardly speak... and we *know* she likes to drink from the washbasin...

But as Timothy says, we want the little swallow to grow up, don't we? And fly, according to his bird book, away to Africa in the autumn? And come back again next year and nest in our roof instead of the starlings? And be a perishing nuisance for evermore, I think despondently. Throwing its fledglings down for me to look after – and I bet they all like egg.

I dare not say this openly, of course. We are all such naturalists now. Solomon, when I left a chicken in the kitchen this morning ready for the oven – and he, with a quick glance over his shoulder, nipped it into the yard – was quite hurt when I said he'd stolen it. Fainted it had, he assured me sorrowfully. He'd taken it out for Air.

Solomon right now is lying in a deckchair, waiting for his tea and swatting – though not, I fear, with the swallow in mind – the gnatflies as they pass. Time we finished writing, he says – and probably he is right. Who, if we told them, would believe any more of our stories? About our getting a mate for Tarzan, for instance, at Timothy's suggestion... and what happened after that. Solomon in any case is tired – and you know who *really* wrote this book? Not me, if you go by his expression. But a big, Seal-Pointed cat.

CATS
IN THE BELFRY

'The most enchanting cat book ever'
Jilly Cooper

DOREEN TOVEY

Cats in the Belfry

Doreen Tovey

£6.99 Pb

1 84024 452 6

'It wasn't, we discovered as the months went by, that Sugieh was particularly wicked. It was just that she was a Siamese.'

Animal lover Doreen and her husband Charles acquire their first Siamese kitten to rid themselves of an invasion of mice. But Sugieh is not just any cat. She's an actress, a prima donna, an iron hand in a delicate, blue-pointed glove. She quickly establishes herself as queen of the house, causing chaos daily by screaming like a banshee, chewing up telegrams, and tearing holes in anything made of wool.

First published over forty years ago, this warm and witty classic tale is a truly enjoyable read for anyone who's ever been owned by a cat.

'If there is a funnier book about cats I for one do not want to read it. I would hurt myself laughing, might even die of laughter'
                                                                    The Scotsman

'Every so often, there comes along a book – or if you're lucky books – which gladden the heart, cheer the soul... Just such books are those written by Doreen Tovey'
                                                                    Cat World

THE
NEW BOY

From the bestselling author of *Cats In The Belfry*

DOREEN TOVEY

The New Boy

Doreen Tovey

£6.99 Pb

1 84024 517 4

'So there we were, driving along with an earth-box, a bag of turkey and, squalling his head off on my knee in Sheba's basket, the new boy.'

The Toveys are no strangers to disaster, particularly the Siamese-related kind, but when their beloved Solomon dies unexpectedly, they're faced with a completely new type of problem – do they find another cat to replace the one they've lost?

The animals always win in the Tovey household and this time is no exception. It is with the interests of Solomon's (very audibly) grieving sister Sheba at heart that Doreen and Charles set off in search of Solomon Secundus, affectionately known as Seeley.

Joined by a myriad of endearing characters, Seeley ensures he's living up to Solomon's standards in just the amount of time it takes to fall in a fishpond. This is an enchanting tale that will tickle your funny bone and tug on your heartstrings all in the same breath.

Chapter One

There was nothing, that last summer, to warn us of the sadness that lay so short a while ahead.

True, Sheba had been ill the previous autumn. 'Kidney trouble' the Vet had diagnosed after examining her. And when he told us gently that she was now an elderly cat, that her kidneys were very much enlarged but that with treatment and careful diet we might, if we were lucky, have her with us for another year – we were numbed at the prospect of the future without her.

For thirteen years life in our West Country cottage had been dominated by a pair of Siamese cats: Sheba, the clever one; tiny, blue-pointed and as fragile as a flower: Solomon, her noisy brother; seal-pointed, huge, our bumble-footed clown.

Every inch of the place held a memory of them doing something. Sheba playing tag with us on the coalhouse roof on a summer's night, for instance. Hanging over the edge bawling she was Here, we weren't to go in without her or the Foxes might Get Her – and then, as we reached up to lift her down, retreating lightheartedly to another corner saying Ha! ha! That one fooled us, didn't it? She wasn't afraid of Foxes...

Or Solomon, dark-backed and seemingly as unmoving as a doorstop, peering stolidly through the gate when he knew we were keeping an eye on him. Always the adventurer was Solomon. Never within our boundaries if he could help it and, on the occasions when we had to go out and were watching him like security guards to make sure he didn't get away (wipe a plate – out to check on him; put away a jug – out to check on him again), there he'd be sitting by the gate. Very ostentatiously With Us. Not a thought in his head about moving. Why on Earth, enquired the set of his back view, were we watching him Like That? And waiting, as well we knew, to vanish like Siamese lightning the moment we took our eyes off him.

One day, of course, we would have to lose them. The one dis-service animals render us is that they don't live as long as we do. But cats live longer than dogs. We'd heard of Siamese of twenty and more. And not only had our two, until Sheba's illness, gone through life with the enthusiasm of eternal kittens, but it seemed such a little while since they had been young.

I could reach out, it seemed, and almost touch them like it. Going down the lane at three months old with their mother and their brothers in the wheelbarrow... all the others in the wheelbarrow that is, and Solomon tagging tearfully along behind.

Lying on our bed at six months old, when Sheba had recently been spayed and, when we switched on the light wondering at the peculiar snicking noises, there was Solomon, mortified at being discovered, helping her by trying to bite her stitches out. The first time we took them to the Siamese cattery at Halstock after their mother had died and, as we left, they'd sat side by side in their big paved run, wistfully watching us go. They had the tips of their tails crossed, like children holding hands to give each other courage. They'd done that, said Mrs Francis, every time they sat out in their run...

Thirteen years had slipped by since then like May mist blown by the wind. The cats were seven when we acquired an eleven months' old donkey and now Annabel was seven herself. As wayward as ever and there was no need to worry about her age, thank goodness. Donkeys live to twenty at least, and we had been told they could live to forty.

I worried about the cats, though. Being the world's worst pessimist I always had done. I worried when they were ill. I worried when they were out of sight. When Solomon was out of sight, at any rate, for Sheba very rarely strayed. I ran like a deer at the sound of a cat-fight, in case the loudest, most urgent of the howls should be (as they usually were) Solomon, having started the fracas, bawling for me to come to the rescue. Sometimes I ran when it wasn't a cat-fight – bursting through the door, shouting 'SOLOMON!' as I went, only to find that it was the boy who lived on the hill practising bird-calls, or visitors to the Valley calling their dogs.

Embarrassing though it was, it didn't really bother me. I would have gone to the ends of the earth to rescue Solomon. To rescue any of them, if it came to that – but particularly Solomon, who was not only more likely to be at the ends of the earth than any of the others, but because for me he was something very special.

I had never, for a moment, taken him for granted. In thirteen years I had never once seen him come round a corner or into a room with that dawdling, elegant walk of his, without marvelling at the perfection of his beauty. He had the proud, high-boned features of the East from which he came. His face shone like dusky silk. And if his slanted, sapphire eyes had faded a little with the years, they were the most loving, communicative eyes I have ever encountered in a cat.

www.summersdale.com